The Hudson River Valley

by William G. Scheller

CHRIS MAYNARD

Photographs by Chris Maynard
unless otherwise credited

American Geographic Publishing

Helena, Montana

William A. Cordingley, Chairman
Rick Graetz, Publisher
Mark Thompson, Director of Publications
Barbara Fifer, Production Manager

Number 2

For Kay

About the author

  William G. Scheller is the author of 11 books and more than 100 magazine articles, including American Geographic Publishing's *New Hampshire: Portrait of the Land and Its People*. Since 1970 he has made his home in Vermont and Massachusetts.

ISBN 0-938314-55-6

© 1988 American Geographic Publishing, P.O. Box 5630, Helena, MT 59604

text © 1988 William G. Scheller

photographs © 1988 Chris Maynard unless otherwise credited

Design by Linda McCray; Steve Morehouse, graphic artist

Printed in Korea by Dong-A Printing Co.

CHRIS MAYNARD PHOTOS BOTH PAGES

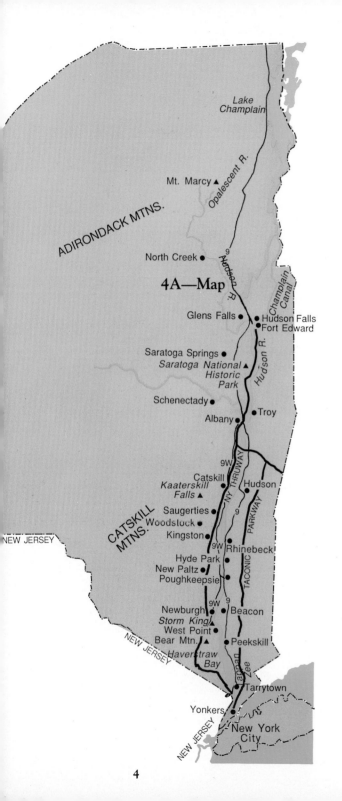

4A—Map

Lake Champlain

Mt. Marcy ▲

Opalescent R.

ADIRONDACK MTNS.

North Creek ●

Hudson R.

Champlain Canal

Glens Falls ● Hudson Falls
Fort Edward

Saratoga Springs ●
Saratoga National Historic Park ▲

Hudson R.

Schenectady ●

Albany ● ● Troy

9W

NY THRUWAY

Catskill ●
Kaaterskill Falls ▲ Hudson ●

9

TACONIC PARKWAY

CATSKILL MTNS.
Saugerties ●
Woodstock ●
Kingston ●

9W

Rhinebeck ●

Hyde Park ●
New Paltz ●
Poughkeepsie ●

9W 9

Newburgh ● ● Beacon
Storm King ▲
West Point ●
Bear Mtn. ▲ ● Peekskill
Haverstraw Bay

Tappan Zee

Tarrytown ●

Yonkers ●

New York City

NEW JERSEY

NEW JERSEY

4

Above: *The Yaddo gardens, open to the public.*
Facing page: *At New Paltz.*

Front cover: *Garrison's Landing.* CHRIS MAYNARD
Page 1: *The Hudson from Bear Mountain Bridge.*
Page 2: *Off Garrison's Landing.*
Page 3: *The 1692 Deyo House at New Paltz.*

CHRIS MAYNARD PHOTOS BOTH PAGES

CONTENTS

PROLOGUE

For the first 20 years of my life I lived within a half-hour's drive of the Hudson River, yet I doubt that I ever thought of it as anything but a natural barrier to be crossed on the way from New Jersey to New York City. It wasn't a river, really; it was the Lincoln or the Holland Tunnel, or the George Washington Bridge. My approach to the river was perpendicular, never parallel, and certainly never at water level.

In the fall of 1985, I made up for those years of ignoring the Hudson by launching a canoe from a pier in lower Manhattan, heading south toward the harbor, and circumnavigating the island. On the face of it, my partner Chris Maynard and I were paddling around Manhattan for Canoe magazine, but if there had been no assignment we would have done it anyway. We were drawn to the notion of seeing the city from the level of the rivers that surround it—but the real epiphany, at the half-way point in our trip, was the broad Hudson at the northern gates of the metropolis.

Now, to circumnavigate Manhattan by heading south from a point at the West Side below Canal Street, you follow the Hudson to the Battery and round the southern prow of the island, turning north into the East River. This we did with the flood tide behind us, according to plan; we not so much paddled as shot up the East and Harlem rivers, heading toward an afternoon landfall at Fort Tryon Park on the northern tip of Manhattan Island. This is where the narrow channel called the Spuyten Duyvil connects the Harlem with the Hudson River, and where we had chosen to camp for the night.

Where can you camp safely in New York? We had scouted the spot. At the mouth of the Spuyten Duyvil there is an abandoned New York Central railroad bridge, pivoted into a permanently open position so that it faces the Hudson and the Palisade cliffs of New Jersey beyond. The stub-end of the bridge was docked neatly into a little triangular pier, standing 10 feet above the water. The only way to reach it was by boat. As the 6 o'clock October dusk gathered, we paddled from the park to the bridge and hauled ourselves, canoe and all, onto the pier. We pitched a tent and made our dinner, the only campers in New York—at least the only ones who had homes to go to. Drizzle had given way to a light mist. We were on the Hudson River.

The Hudson at the northern extreme of Manhattan is hardly a city river, especially at night. Behind us, high up, was the drone of traffic on the Henry Hudson Bridge, and to the north were the lights of a residential section of the Bronx. But when we looked south toward Times Square we saw nothing but the darkness of Fort Tryon Park and the suspended arc of lights that marked the George Washington Bridge. The Palisades across the river, part of an interstate park, were nothing but a black shape above the water. The Hudson River here begins to broaden. Already at least a mile across, it swells not many miles north into the virtual lake called the Tappan Zee. All this expanse of water was gray and soundless in the gathering dusk, looking much the same as it did 400 years ago.

Then a light appeared to separate from the jeweled span of the Tappan Zee Bridge, far to the north, and drifted toward our camp. It was fixed to the mast of a sailing vessel. When the boat fell even with our westward line of sight, we could see by its white sails against the black Palisades that it was a single-masted sloop, heading for the harbor. Soon the last daylight failed and the sails were gone; only the drifting lamp remained. The only sound was the lap of the Hudson on our pilings.

"Listen, " I said to Chris. "The crew is singing in Dutch."

Most American places do not feel haunted. Or, to put it in natural rather than supernatural terms, they do not play upon the imagination in such a way as to produce near-tangible impressions of ages and people long gone. Our natural landscapes seldom strike us so, unless they bear reminders of the ancient epic of Indians and pioneers; and our larger cities are so busy with their daily reinvention of themselves that hardly any necessary touchstones for remembrance of things past still exist. Once in awhile a construction crew will find the shards of an ale jar in the excavation for a Wall Street tower, and a window will open on tavern life in New Amsterdam. But it will close just as quickly, and New York—as would Chicago or Atlanta or Seattle—will go right on living in the present day.

The Hudson River Valley is a great exception to this American rule. The windows on all its eras are nearly always open, so that despite whatever modern progress its communities may make, it is never difficult for a visitor to conjure the faces and voices of the valley's past. This is the river of Franklin Roosevelt, of Frederick Church and Benedict Arnold and "Gentleman Johnny" Burgoyne. Washington Irving owns it still, and Hendrick Hudson forever sails upstream toward its hidden heart. It is the Hudson itself that brings all these ghosts to life. Like the sea it is immutable, no matter what we might do to its shoreline or the chemistry of its water. Broad, silent, and powerful, the Hudson flows through time as easily as through the counties of eastern New York State, and in the mind's eye it can float a tall Dutch ship as easily as a little green canoe.

Most American places do not feel haunted…   CHRIS MAYNARD

The Saratoga Battlefield.

CHRIS MAYNARD

Throughout much of its length, the Hudson is not so much a river as an estuary. It is a drowned tidal river, with scarcely more than a five foot drop in its level between Albany and the Battery on Manhattan, 150 miles to the south. The tides affect the river as far north as Troy, and it is only the Hudson's own current that prevents salt water from reaching even farther than its northern limit at Marlboro, just south of Poughkeepsie.

Part of the Hudson Valley can actually be classified as a fjord, one of two on the eastern seaboard of the United States. The other, Somes Sound near Bar Harbor on Maine's Mount Desert Island, is vastly smaller and much more in keeping with the common notion of fjords as influenced by postcard scenery of Scandinavia and British Columbia. The section of the Hudson that fits the fjord description extends south to New York City from Hudson Gorge, the narrow place in the river that begins below Newburgh Bay and ends at Haverstraw Bay and the broad, lakelike Tappan Zee. A fjord is nothing more than a riverbed that has been gorged deeper than sea level by a glacier, and later filled with the inrushing ocean. That is what happened here, after southbound Pleistocene ice covered the Hudson Highlands and Palisades, piling even higher than the summits of Storm King and Bear Mountain.

But the estuarial Hudson and the Hudson as fjord only represent the dramatic concluding miles of a river that begins far to the north, in the shadow of Mt. Marcy in the Adirondack Mountains. From its source to the town of Hudson Falls, where it begins to flow due south, the Hudson is a country stream, indistinguishable from countless others fed by the melting snows of the Adirondacks. The young Hudson is what topographers call a "radial" stream, abruptly bending from one direction to another as required by the regional system of geologic faults. Only after Hudson Falls does the river itself become a dominant geographic feature of the landscape, as it flows along a continuation of the Champlain Valley between the Taconic Mountains, to the east, and the Catskills and Shawangunks, to the west.

Geology and topography of the Hudson Valley and adjacent mountains

The Hudson River rises in the east-central Adirodacks, a region geologically characterized by Precambrian granites and the Grenville strata of gneiss, quartzite and limestone, all easily more than half a billion years old. Near Glens Falls, where the river broadens markedly just prior to turning sharply southward, it enters into a region whose primary rock is shale, limestone, sandstone and chert laid down as sediment during the Ordovician period, some 425 to 500 million years ago. Farther south, the Hudson Highlands are also Precambrian, consisting of granite and granite-injected crystalline rocks thrust upward as block faults through more recently formed sedimentary strata. For all their modern-day majesty, the Highlands are but the roots of a long-vanished range of much higher mountains, worn down by erosion. The river is flanked to the east by the Taconic Range, an extension of the Berkshires of Massachusetts and northwestern Connecticut that was created by folding and was also once far loftier; and

9

CHRIS MAYNARD PHOTOS BOTH PAGES

on the west by the Catskills, the elevated eastern margin of the valley-riven Allegheny Plateau. The sedimentary deposits of transient ancient seas, and the later gorging and plowing action of the Pleistocene glaciers, refined the contours of the Hudson Valley and gave it the appearance we are familiar with today.

Along with such free standing promontories as Storm King and Anthony's Nose, both of which sentinel the river as it flows through Hudson Gorge, perhaps the most striking natural features of the immediate Hudson Shoreline are the towering black cliffs called the Palisades. The Palisades extend for more than 40 miles along the river's west bank, starting in the vicinity of Weehawken, New Jersey and tapering off north of the Tappan Zee.

The loftiest and most abruptly vertical section of the Palisades, near the New York-New Jersey border, best displays the columnar, prism-like structure that makes the cliffs distinctive. Their appearance here is a direct clue to their origins: the Palisades were formed nearly 200 million years ago when molten rock irrupted into fissures in the compacted sediment of the Newark Basin. The magma cooled and solidified underground, transforming into a basaltlike substance called diabase and marked by coarse, visible crystals of feldspar and pyroxene. (Farther west, in what is now New Jersey, the low mountain ridges of the Watchungs formed in much the same way. But since the Watchung basalt broke the surface, it cooled more quickly, creating a denser texture in which little mineral crystallization can be noticed.)

As the Palisades diabase cooled and hardened underground, it contracted and splintered vertically to create the appearance of great, elongated crystals clustered in unbroken rows. After millions of years of sediment erosion the cliffs finally stood exposed, and were so suggestive of a dark, impenetrable forest that the Indians called them *Wee-awk-en*, "the rocks that look like trees." Europeans were drawn to a different metaphor, seeing a resemblance in the cliffs to the military fortification made up of sharpened stakes, called a "palisade." Both terms survive—Weehawken as the name of a New Jersey town at the western terminus of the Lincoln Tunnel, and Palisades as the name of the cliffs themselves and the interstate park that encompasses much of them.

Farther west, the southwest-to-northeast ridge of the Shawangunks—the beloved "Gunks" of generations of rock climbers—represent a different process of mountain building. Like the Taconics and the main formation of the Hudson

Highlands, the Shawangunks are the roots of long-eroded ancient mountains, which in this case were folded and broken under intense subterranean pressure to create the challenging walls of the present-day range.

The first human inhabitants

Just as we associate South Dakota with the Sioux or Arizona with the Navajo and Apaches, so too does the state of New York have a broad and general association with a particular tribe of native Americans—in this instance, the tough and tenacious Iroquois. But despite their dominance over most of what was to become New York, the Iroquois were not the first people to hold sway over the area, nor did they ever constitute the main native population of the Hudson Valley.

The Archaic peoples, paleoindians, came first, followed by Laurentian groups that descended into New York from the St. Lawrence Valley. Successive centuries brought the Vine Valley culture from the west, with its pottery and polished implements suggestive of the leisure that produces craftsmanship; then the Mound Builders and the agricultural Owasco people. By the time Europeans first arrived in New York in significant numbers, in the early 17th century, the pre-eminent tribal groups in the Hudson Valley and its environs were the Algonquins. The Algonquins were descendants of people who had migrated eastward in pursuit of a legendary "water that flows two ways" and found their

Above: *Storm King is seen to the right of picture.*
Left: *Rock climbers in the Shawangunks.*
Facing page: *This view of the Palisades explains why roads have "Fallen Rock Zones."*

11

CHRIS MAYNARD PHOTOS BOTH PAGES

promised land along a river ruled by both its current and the tides. On the west bank of the river and in New Jersey lived the Lenni Lenape tribes, generically dubbed the "Delawares" by the whites—Raritans, Hackensacks, Haverstraws, Catskills and others. (The tribal designations reflect Dutch and English nomenclature, not that of the Indians themselves.) On the Hudson's east bank were Manhattans and Wappingers, while farther north the Mohicans—Algonquins also—laid claim to the hills that circle Lake George and Lake Champlain.

The Lenni Lenape and the other Algonquin tribes of eastern New York State were generally peaceful; whatever belligerent impulses they once might have possessed had long since been subdued by that great tranquilizer, prolonged prosperity. The river itself was their prosperity: today when we follow the fortunes of the Hudson's shad and striped bass as if we were rooting for piscine underdogs, it is hard to imagine the wealth of fish and shellfish that the estuary once harbored, and the game that teemed in the forested highlands. Not merely hunters and gatherers, the Hudson Valley Algonquins also tilled the soil, cultivating the corn, beans and squash that likewise filled the gardens of the earliest white settlers. They grew tobacco and smoked it in clay pipes.

Unfortunately, peaceful intentions and peace are two different things. During the final century in which the Indians had North America's middle Atlantic region to themselves, Iroquois tribes began to press in upon the Algonquian homelands between the Great Lakes and the Hudson from the north as well as from the south and southwest. The northern Iroquois settled along the valley of the Mohawk, the Hudson's principal tributary, while those from the south established themselves in what is now the western arm of New York state between lakes Erie and Ontario. The Iroquois had stamina, an appetite for warfare and, above all, a will to dominate that enabled them to subsume internecine rivalries for the benefit of all their number. They were the Prussians of native America, and through a series of artful compromises that would have done Bismarck proud they managed, in about 1570, to create the mighty Confederacy of Five Nations: Senecas, Cayugas, Onondagas, Oneidas and Mohawks, united around a strong common law and base of power in the Finger Lakes region. This was the Indian war machine that wrought such terrible havoc upon the settlements of New France in the St. Lawrence Valley, after the French under Champlain made a fateful decision to side with the Iroquois' enemies. It was also the great nemesis of the Algonquin tribes of the Hudson Valley, whom they harassed not so much in pursuit of total territorial domination as for booty and slaves. Of all the Algonquin component tribes, only the Mohicans were strong enough to offer more than token resistance to the Iroquois.

The European discovery of the Hudson

The first European explorer of record to have visited the Hudson River was not the man for whom it was named. In 1524, the Italian navigator Giovanni da Verrazano sailed his Dauphin into lower New York Bay, where, as he later wrote, "a mighty deep-mouthed river ran into the sea." Verrazano sent out a small boat with an exploring party to ascend the river, and from the captain's subsequent account we may infer that the boat reached the broad inner harbor below Governor's Island and the southern tip of Manhattan. There Verrazano's men were approached by curious Indians in their canoes, but before they could make contact with the natives the wind reversed and they were forced back to the Dauphin. The captain made no further attempts to venture inland. Consequently, his name today is attached to the bridge across the Narrows at the entrance to the harbor and not to the great river that empties there.

Several other 16th-century mariners could have been the formal "discoverers" of the Hudson River, but like Verrazano they failed to systematically explore the channel beyond its mouth and left only meager accounts of their travels, if they left them at all. In 1525, one year after Verrazano's voyage, a Portuguese captain named Estavan Gomez entered the Narrows while cruising along the North American coast under the Spanish flag. Toward the end of the century, Dutch traders became increasingly familiar with the area around New York harbor, and by that time the upper reaches of the Hudson Valley had most likely been visited by French fur traders working their way south into the wilderness from their outposts along the St. Lawrence River. The year 1609 found the greatest French explorer of all, Samuel de Champlain, making his way southward along what was to be Lake Champlain into territory that was not far from the Hudson's headwaters. It was on this expedition that Champlain shot and killed an Iroquois chief, an act that touched off the century and a half of bloody enmity between New France and the Five Nation Confederacy.

In that same year of 1609, it fell upon an English adventurer in the employ of the Dutch East India Company to finally settle the place of the still mysterious river in the muddled geography of the New World. Henry Hudson, or Hendrick Hudson as he was called by his Dutch employers, had been engaged to find that navigational chimera of the centuries, the Northwest Passage to the Orient. His instructions had called for an initial exploration in the vicinity of the Arctic Island of Novaya Zemlya, but as his crew grew mutinous when faced with the ice and cold of the northern sea, Hudson steered his 80-ton ship Half Moon south toward the coast of North America. (Mutiny was to finally prove Hudson's undoing, when on a subsequent voyage his crew set him and his son adrift on the dreary, frigid expanse of what has since been called Hudson Bay.)

The Half Moon passed Cape Cod early in August, and three weeks later had reached the Chesapeake Bay. Entry into

13

CHRIS MAYNARD PHOTOS BOTH PAGES

From Bear Mountain Bridge.

between the headlands charted by Verrazano 85 years earlier, Hudson dropped anchor in Newark Bay. Here he and his men caught fish for provisions and made their first contact with the Indians. Relations were cordial at first—the natives gave the sailors tobacco and dried currants—but within a few days an altercation resulted in the death from an arrow wound of an English crewman. After a week of making ready for further exploration and developing a more circumspect approach to dealings with the Lenni Lenape (two hostages were taken on board, but they escaped north of West Point), the party was ready to head north in the *Half Moon* to see if they had indeed stumbled upon the shortcut to China.

The first day's sailing brought Hudson and his men to a point roughly three miles above the northern tip of Manhattan Island; it would have been during that run that they first beheld the strange, beetling cliffs of the Palisades and passed the Spuyten Duyvil, now spanned at great height by the Henry Hudson Bridge (and at water level by an old railroad bridge beloved by certain canoeists). On the following day, September 14, Hudson's hopes that the river would prove a passage to the Orient must have soared as the *Half Moon* entered the broad expanse of the Tappan Zee and Haverstraw Bay. But by the end of that day's sail the river narrowed again, as the little Dutch ship passed between the abrupt slopes and domes of the Hudson Highlands. That night, the *Half Moon* anchored on the west bank of the Hudson Gorge, near the place where the U.S. Military Academy stands today.

"The fifteenth, in the morning was misty until the Sun arose: then it cleared," wrote Robert Juet, one of Henry Hudson's officers, in the diary he kept of the voyage. "So we weighed with the wind at south, and ran up the river twenty leagues, passing by high mountains." And so the Catskills entered recorded history, as the *Half Moon* glided along Newburgh Bay under clear skies and favorable winds. Within three days the site of Albany was reached. This was as far north as the *Half Moon* was to travel; on September 20, Hudson sent the ship's boat with a party of five men upstream as far as the mouth of the Mohawk River near present-day Waterford. By now the captain was convinced he had not found the Northwest Passage (Champlain, working south as far as Lake George, had come to the same conclusion), and three days later he began to retrace his river route. By the 26th the *Half Moon* had cleared New York harbor and entered the open Atlantic, after a downstream voyage marred by further

the bay was thwarted by a storm. Using a map given to him by Capt. John Smith, Hudson then piloted his vessel north to Delaware Bay, which he discounted as the western outlet of a passage to Cathay, and cruised along the sandy shore of New Jersey until he reached the Narrows on September 3. Passing conflict with the Indians and the deaths of several natives by gunshot and cannon fire. At Albany one old chief had met with an even more potent weapon in the white man's arsenal, when Henry Hudson had gotten him drunk. The Indians' gift of tobacco was to be repaid in kind.

Henry Hudson never again saw the great river, nor was he ever to be aware of its being named for him. Throughout their six-decade tenure in the valley, the Dutch called the river "Mauritius" after Prince Maurice of the Netherlands. It was the English, after they seized control of New Amsterdam and the valley lands, who named the Hudson after their countryman.

The Hudson becomes a Dutch river

Despite the less than propitious beginnings of relations between the Dutch and Indians for which the *Half Moon*'s captain and crew had been responsible, another vessel from the Netherlands called at the mouth of the Hudson within a year to trade with the Indians. This was the first of several annual commercial voyages. In 1613, a party led by Adrian Block and Hendrick Christiaenson became the first Netherlanders to over-winter in the new territory; they sailed inland as far as Castle Island, near Albany, where they built a rudimentary, palisaded trading post called Fort Nassau. Another post was built nearby in the following year, but 1614 was more important as the year in which the New Netherland Company was chartered. Its purpose was to organize a monopoly on the fur trade along the river, and toward this end it sponsored several lucrative expeditions and brought the first small groups of settlers to the valley.

After Fort Nassau was destroyed in a flood in 1617, it was replaced by a larger port, a fortified village called Fort Orange that stood on the higher ground where the city of Albany later would be built. Although the fur trade had been the primary reason for the construction of Fort Nassau, the new settlement soon began to attract Walloon refugees from Holland, who initially farmed in the immediate area and later moved downriver to another tiny Dutch colony that was forming on the cluster of islands at the mouth of the Hudson.

The settlements at Fort Orange, at Manhattan and at "Breuckelen" at the western tip of Long Island were the result of the formation of the Dutch West India Company, a government-organized, stockholder-owned monopoly

An abandoned armory near the Newburgh-Beacon Bridge off Storm King.

corporation conceived as a successor to the New Netherland Company. Chartered in 1621, the West India Company organized the migration of the Walloon refugees, French-speaking Protestants from southern Holland (now Belgium) who had been subjected to Spanish Catholic persecution during the Netherlands' struggle with Spain. Thirty families of Walloons arrived at New York harbor in the ship *New Netherland* in the late spring of 1624. Most of them continued upriver to Fort Orange, while some dispersed to the Delaware and Connecticut valleys. Only eight men remained on the narrow, forested island that thrust its southern tip prow-like into Upper New York Bay. They purchased that island from the Indians—not the same Indians, the story has it, who were its principal inhabitants—in what has since become the most celebrated real estate transaction in history. Sixty guilders (about $24) worth of trinkets changed hands, and "Mannahatta" became the property of the West India

Settlement by Dutch colonists gave the Hudson Valley a character different from New England's.

West Point as seen from Storm King.

Company and the site of New Amsterdam. Such was the art of the deal in 1624.

Within a year, more settlers arrived at New Amsterdam. A fort was built, and Dutch authority was now anchored at both ends of the navigable portion of the Hudson. It had been only five years since the *Mayflower* pilgrims had staked out their settlement on the shores of Massachusetts Bay; the town of Boston would not be founded for another five years. It would be nearly six decades before William Penn would start to lay the grid of Philadelphia. Of the three rival metropolises of the

Northeast, New York can justly claim to having been there first.

Additional groups of colonists arrived at the mouth of the Hudson during the latter 1620s, and the first importations of livestock from the mother country were made. The first farms were hewn from the wilderness along the banks of the Hudson, many of them on Manhattan Island itself. It is a Dutch word for small farm, *bouwerie*, that survives in a different spelling as the name of a less than bucolic New York City street and neighborhood; this particular farm was the property of none other than Peter Stuyvesant, the last governor of New Amsterdam. (The Dutch word for farmer is *boer*, a term with which the world would become familiar in a far distant geographical context centuries later.)

In order to stabilize the Hudson Valley colony by encouraging farmers to settle along the river, the West India Company in 1629 undertook an experiment called the "Charter of Freedoms and Exemptions." This was the patroon system, under which a large hereditary estate would be granted to any company stockholder or "patroon" (patron) agreeing to sponsor at least 50 settlers on his grant within four years of its receipt. All of the valley was to be divided, with the exemption of Manhattan Island, which would remain the monopoly's corporate property. It was an essentially feudal arrangement, similar in many respects to the French seigneurial system instituted in Quebec during the 17th century. Like the French, the Dutch colonists had to face the fact that fur traders do not make for a stable colony readily defensible against foreign powers; they take their profits and go home without tilling the soil, raising families and setting down roots. The patroon system was a means of delegating the responsibility for settlement. It gave to the Hudson Valley a character essentially different from that of New England, whose villages constituted a collection of semi-autonomous democracies; only in the South did anything like such a feudal society exist, although of course the existence of chattel slavery made the Southern plantations a different matter entirely. (The Dutch held black slaves, but despite their importance on some large estates they were never the long-term foundation of agricultural economy as in the South.)

Short of a handful of Texas ranches, there is almost nothing on the modern real estate landscape to compare in

CHRIS MAYNARD PHOTOS BOTH PAGES

Above: *A Victorian home in Rhinebeck.*
Left: *Washington's 1781 headquarters in Newburgh.*

17

Looking across Newburgh to the Hudson from the porch of Crawford House, built in 1834.

Rensselaer, was named by him Rensselaerswyck. Van Rensselaer never crossed the Atlantic to visit his vast fiefdom, which was roughly centered about Fort Orange, but he occupied himself diligently in milking the land, the river and his tenants for as many guilders as they could yield. He had his agents buy surrounding property so that his holdings eventually far exceeded the amount nominally permissible under the charter and even attempted, robber-baron style, to dictate contractual terms to shippers operating on what he considered his section of the Hudson. Eventually, Rensselaerswyck amounted to a jurisdiction all its own, coexistent with the settlements at New Amsterdam and Fort Orange. It survived to the American Revolution and beyond.

The hereditary landholdings of the Hudson Valley, whether enormous patroonships such as the van Rensselaer family's or the smaller manors of patentees such as the Philipses, Cortlandts and Beekmans, were the cornerstones of a system in which tenant farming was the norm, as opposed to the New England concept of independent yeoman farmers each in possession of his own land. The Dutch West India Company itself was a reactionary and stifling influence, as far as the aspirations of individual colonists might have been concerned; it sharply limited opportunities for trade and speculation in property, controlled all imports and exports, and levied heavy taxes on the settlers of the Hudson Valley and New Amsterdam. The management of the colony was a continuing story of short-term profit seeking and heavy-handed administration, the latter perhaps best represented by the paternal director general of New Netherland, Peter Stuyvesant. In August of 1664, when an English fleet under Col. Richard Nicolls sailed through the Narrows and demanded that Stuyvesant surrender the colony to Great Britain, the director's fractious subjects offered him so little support that he immediately agreed to the British terms. The special privileges of the valley's great landholders would survive for nearly another 200 years, and eventually the colonists would chafe as much under British rule as they had under Dutch. But for the time being, the removal of the West India Company from their lives was a welcome turn of events.

The British colonial era

When Col. Nicolls sailed into ship's gun range of New Amsterdam and took the colony without firing a shot, he was enforcing a British policy dating back to 1621, when James I of

size with the Dutch patroonships in colonial America. They were permitted to extend for 16 miles along the river if only one side was to be settled, or eight miles if both shores were to be included. Their east-west dimensions could range "as far inland as the situation of the occupants will permit." A piece of property extending along a 16-mile length of riverfront and running 10 miles into the interior amounts to over 102,000 acres—and some of the Dutch landholdings were even larger. With them came the responsibility to pay the Indians for the title. They also meant freedom from land taxes for a period of eight years (10 years for the patroon's tenants)—the "exemptions" referred to in the West India Company's charter.

Investors originally applied for and received six patroonships, two each on the Delaware, Connecticut and Hudson rivers. Of the six only one remained viable by 1635— the largest, obtained by Amsterdam jeweler Kilaen van

England claimed sovereignty over the Hudson Valley by right of "occupancy." The reference was more to discovery than to actual occupancy—John Cabot having laid vague claim to the entire North Atlantic coast of the New World for Britain at the close of the 15th century—but the intent was practical and clear: the possessor of the expanding colonies in Virginia and New England was not going to allow the Netherlands to occupy the finest natural harbor on the coast and the great river that led inland to rich farmlands and fur trade wealth.

New Netherland was given as a patent to the brother of King Charles II, James, Duke of York. New Amsterdam was thus rechristened New York, and all along the Hudson Valley English place names supplanted those of the Dutch. Fort Orange and its companion town of Beverwyck became Albany; Rondout became Kingston; and the Mauritius River was given the name of its discoverer, Henry Hudson. (The Dutch nomenclature was restored when the Netherlands recaptured the colony in 1673, only to disappear again when British rule was permanently reasserted by treaty in the following year.) Despite the new political order, Dutch cultural influences in the Hudson Valley remained pervasive— and not merely through the survival of the tenant-farming system and the names of the colony's smaller communities. The Dutch Reformed Church continued as a leading religious institution, and indeed has many members in southern New York State and northern New Jersey today.

Architectural historians recognize "Dutch Colonial" as an important local vernacular style, characterized by gambrel roofs, solid brownstone construction, and features such as the "Dutch door" designed to let in breezes while keeping out livestock, and a "stoop" (Dutch stoep) to sit on during the summer. Dutch topographical terms abound to this day — throughout the Hudson Valley, we encounter the word "kill" for a stream or creek; "clove" for a deep vale in the mountains; "hook" for a narrow projection of land into a body of water; and "zee" (sea) as in Tappan Zee. Even our food words have been influenced: "cookie" and "cruller" are both borrowings from the Dutch. As for folklore, we need only look as far as the writings of Washington Irving, which in large part distill the legends and informal history of the Hudson Valley in the days of New Netherland. (The influence of later German settlers, according to some scholars, is also evident in Irving's work.)

Summer begins to fade on a Prattsville-area farm.

But the new British masters of New York had laid claim to far more than a quaint backwater of transplanted Dutch language and culture. Along with the tremendous strategic advantage of the harbor and the Northeast's most important inland waterway, they had come into possession of a thriving colony of farmers and tradesmen of assorted nationalities— German, French, Swedish, Danish, Irish and even Jewish immigrants had already begun to migrate to New York and the string of upriver settlements. Praised by English

19

JIM CRONK

"What was good enough for my fathers..." near Prattsville.

and wild grapes. What they did not always find was ready access to free land for farming, since the English made the mistake of perpetuating the Dutch practice of making enormous hereditary land grants. Whatever use the manorial system may once have had in the opening of the century, it began to prove self-defeating in an era when most immigrants wished to start off with small but unencumbered holdings of their own. The lords of the Hudson were not only an obstacle to the free ownership of land, they often were ready exploiters of immigrant labor. Robert Livingston, a Scot who had cleverly married into the van Rensselaer family and built an estate to rival Rensselaerswyck, grew even richer on the labor of a large group of Germans from the Rhineland-Palatinate who had come to New York to escape oppression in their own country.

Like the other immigrant groups, the Germans eventually worked themselves into the social fabric of the Hudson Valley, settling communities such as Rhinebeck, on the river's east bank north of Poughkeepsie and the towns along the Catskills' Schoharie Creek. New Englanders, meanwhile, settled other locations east of the Hudson, while Scotch and Scotch-Irish immigrants helped to develop the west bank. Huguenots who had come from France by way of Germany founded New Paltz, where their handsome stone houses still stand. The proliferation of new settlements in parts of the valley inaccessible to direct river traffic was partly the result of a major innovation of the British era, the building of roads. Under the Dutch regime the ubiquitous river sloops provided virtually the only means of cargo and passenger transport; consequently, towns and farms were concentrated along the Hudson. The British in the 18th century built King's Highways along both the east and west banks of the river, and these thoroughfares were fed in turn by improved capillary roads that supplanted the wagon tracks of the Dutch and the footpaths of the Indians. New York could now communicate with Albany by road or by water, or with New England communities by means of the rudimentary Boston Post Road (the name survives along some sections of U.S. Route 1 near the border of New York's Westchester County and Connecticut) as well as by ship traffic along Long Island Sound. What was happening, in effect, was that the burgeoning English colony along the Hudson and at its mouth was being integrated with Britain's territories to the north and south. It was an imperfect union, with people still identifying themselves as New Yorkers or New Englanders rather than citizens of a larger entity,

newcomers as everything from a "terrestrial Canaan" to "a climate of sweet and wholesome breath," the Hudson Valley began to attract further waves of immigrants: the population of the entire colony of New York grew from 8,000 in 1667 to 168,000 on the eve of the American Revolution a century later. Those who came found rich soil, ample populations of fish and game, and a back-country Eden of chestnuts, berries but the foundations nevertheless were being laid for the sense of cohesion that would see the colonists through their great effort of rebellion near the century's end.

But first there were the French to take care of. Great Britain in the first half of the 18th century was only one of two major powers with a foothold in the northeastern corner of the American continent, and peace between them prevailed far less than war. What American history remembers as the French and Indian War was only the final and climactic struggle in nearly a century of sporadic conflict between the two colonial powers, much of which centered on the upper Hudson Valley.

The showdown began in 1689 with King William's War. In the following year the French and their Indian allies destroyed Schenectady, and the residents of the upper valley feared that Albany might be next. Had the town at the head of navigation fallen, the Hudson might have served as a direct route of French attack on the prosperous villages and towns to the south. That the French did not press upon Albany was largely due to the ability of the English to hold the allegiance of the old enemies of the French, the Iroquois. The Iroquois alliance with the English proved more tenuous during the later phases of the struggle, although the Five Nation Confederacy was always at least neutral and never actively took the side of the French. During new eruptions of warfare in the first decade of the 18th century and again in the 1740s, Albany again avoided being the target of a direct attack—in no small part because of the trading relationship the town enjoyed with Montreal. The events of the French and Indian War of the 1750s and 1760s were largely played out to the north and west of the Hudson Valley proper; the nearest action was the fall of Ticonderoga and Crown Point, on the height of land between Lake Champlain and Lake George. But by prying the French grip from these two north-south waterways and from their defensive posts along the Mohawk, the British and colonial forces finally enabled the Hudson to function as the trunk of a vast system of commerce unhindered by political or military conflict.

There was, of course, one interruption—the Revolutionary War. In New York State as in New England, the roots of the eventual struggle for independence lay in an antipathy that dated back to the 1680s between royal governors and the people's elected representatives. But in

New York the situation was further complicated by the continual chafing of tenant farmers under the manorial system of the great Hudson Valley estates. Oddly enough, when the rebellion finally came it created no neat division of sympathies between the propertied classes and their tenants. Many manor-holders remained loyal to Britain—some 40,000 Tories exiled themselves from the colony and state of New York during and after the war—but the wealthiest families of all, the Livingstons and van Rensselaers, sided with the rebel cause. "Class traitors," they were called by some of their peers. The phrase would echo over a century and a half later when another scion of the Hudson aristocracy, Franklin D. Roosevelt, fell afoul of conservative business interests during the Great Depression.

Several of the earliest acts of defiance against British rule in the 13 colonies took place in the Hudson Valley. There were Stamp Act riots in 1765, one of which led to the

The view of the Hudson afforded from the Livingston estate, Clermont.

21

Above: On the second-floor porch at the Adelphi Hotel, Saratoga Springs.
Facing page: Part of the massive chain stretched across the Hudson during the Revolutionary War to prevent British ships from going north of West Point.

constitution was adopted early the following year, with the new governor and assembly convening in Kingston. The British held the town of New York and would remain there until the formal end of the war in 1783.

The American Revolution

Nearly one third of all engagements of the American Revolution were fought in New York State, and of these a sizeable portion took place in the Hudson Valley. The opening encounters, in the fall of 1776, did not go well for the Continental Army. That October found George Washington and his men camped out at Harlem Heights, near the northern end of Manhattan Island. They were chased from that position by the British under Gen. Howe, but made good their escape to White Plains and hence crossed the Hudson to Fort Lee, New Jersey. The only remaining Manhattan bastion of the colonial forces, Fort Washington (at present-day 183rd Street), fell to a force of British and Hessians the following month.

The fort's capturers used its cannon to shell Washington's position at Fort Lee, while Lord Cornwallis crossed the Hudson to the north. Fort Lee was quickly abandoned, and the Continental Army began its great strategic retreat across New Jersey.

The Continentals, however, still held the Hudson Valley to the north. The major American stronghold was at West Point, where an unusual but ultimately successful defense was put in place in 1778 to keep British warships from moving upriver. This defense was a massive iron chain, with links weighing 300 pounds apiece, that was floated into place on barges and secured on either shore of the Hudson at West Point and Constitution Island. Had Benedict Arnold been successful in his traitorous attempt to hand over West Point to the British, he would have cut the chain as part of the arrangement; as it was, the iron barrier stayed in place until it was disassembled in 1783 and no hostile ships ascended toward Newburgh, Kingston and Albany.

The Hudson Valley's most decisive campaign had already been waged in 1777, the year before the West Point chain was forged. It centered on the most ambitious of Britain's attempts to divide the New England states from those in the Middle Atlantic region, and underscored the importance of the Hudson River as a fulcrum of military strategy.

The British goal in the summer of 1777 was to isolate New England from New York by means of a three-pronged attack.

destruction of a British officer's Hudson River estate. When the hated tax on tea was levied, mobs protested with destruction or seizure of tea in Kinderhook and New York City. And in May of 1775, just after the battles of Lexington and Concord but more than 13 months prior to the signing of the Declaration of Independence, more than 200 anti-British farmers and small tradesmen met at Coxsackie to sign a proclamation calling for self-rule. Official agreement with these sympathies was not long in coming. A provincial congress was formed, which ratified the 1776 Declaration of Independence within five days of its adoption. A state

General John Burgoyne was to follow the Champlain and Hudson valleys south from Canada, while Col. Barry St. Leger's orders were to depart from Lake Ontario and fall upon Albany by way of the Mohawk Valley. The strategy called for Gen. Howe to meet with Burgoyne and St. Leger after moving up the Hudson from New York.

The grand, symmetrical scheme was elegantly simple on paper, but its execution was a disaster. St. Leger's eastward advance was stopped at Fort Stanwix in August, and Howe's northward thrust never began. Having received no specific orders, Howe took it upon himself to move his army south and attack Philadelphia instead. "Gentleman Johnny" Burgoyne made his move south from Canada but was delayed by a defeat at Bennington (a battle commemorated by a monument in Vermont although actually fought across the border in Walloomsac, New York) before taking up positions against the Americans near Saratoga in September. The battles waged there on September 19 and October 7 led to Burgoyne's defeat and encirclement, and the surrender of his forces on October 17. In many respects, Saratoga was the turning point of the war; it convinced the French to enter on the colonists' side and left the Americans in firm possession of the Hudson Valley. Following the final surrender of the British under Cornwallis at Yorktown in 1781, Washington came north and made his headquarters on the Hudson at Newburgh. He entered the town of New York in November of 1783, immediately after the British evacuated under the terms of the Treaty of Paris. Thus it happened that the final triumphal act of the American commander in the revolution was to raise the new nation's flag over what was to become its finest commercial asset in the years ahead: the old Dutch town whose broad river highway to the interior and magnificent harbor were to make it the greatest port in the world.

The 19th century's river of commerce

New York is the only state that touches directly on two of the Great Lakes—Ontario and Erie—and the Atlantic Ocean. Just as important, it possesses in the Hudson River a natural means of access to its heartland, which was a giant first step in any plan to link the ocean with the inland seas. By the beginning of the 19th century, sloops and larger craft had borne commerce up and down the river. Soon, though, the

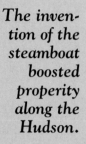

The invention of the steamboat boosted properity along the Hudson.

Lock E-2 of the Erie Canal, at Waterford.

It was ironic that the canal project had originally been opposed by political and mercantile interests in New York City. Like the merchants of Salem and Boston, those in New York City believed that their commercial future lay on the high seas rather than in a ditch leading to the wilderness. But once the canal was finished in 1825, New York began its inexorable climb to the leading position among America's cities; the old New England ports could not compete against a town that stood to benefit from so efficient a conduit of emigration and trade. Buffalo and the midwestern settlements beyond were opened up by people who passed through New York and the towns along the Hudson, and they sent their raw materials back to the great river valley for processing, manufacture and shipping to the outside world.

Prosperity along the Hudson received a further boost with the invention of the steamboat. Experiments with steam propulsion of riverboats had begun during the closing years of the 18th century, with some success achieved along the Delaware River between Pennsylvania and New Jersey by an entrepreneur named John Fitch. History, nevertheless, has chosen to honor Robert Fulton as the inventor of the steamboat—a fact generally conceded to have been a public relations coup on the part of Fulton's partner and father-in-law, Robert Livingston of the manorial Hudson Valley Livingstons. The *Clermont*, which Fulton first demonstrated on the river in 1807, was named after Livingston's estate.

Robert Livingston, who at the time of the *Clermont's* maiden voyage held the now-defunct office of chancellor of New York State, had more than simple patronage in mind when he backed Robert Fulton's efforts. Like his empire-building ancestor who had assembled the Livingston holdings in the valley, he looked to profit from the traffic on the river. Toward this end he got the state legislature to grant him and Fulton a steamboat monopoly on New York waters, interpreted as extending right up to the Jersey side of the harbor. The *Clermont* was followed by five other Fulton boats during the inventor's lifetime (he died in 1815, two years after Livingston), and the monopoly held. If you wanted to make the 36-hour, $7 trip from New York to Albany, or any part thereof, you did so on a Fulton-Livingston steamboat or one licensed by them.

Such a situation couldn't last. Population and traffic along the river was growing too fast for a small fleet of steamboats operated by a single exclusive concern, and too many other smart

Hudson would carry people and cargoes bound for points separated by far more distance than that separating Albany from New York. On the Fourth of July in 1817, Gov. DeWitt Clinton turned the first shovelful of earth for the Erie Canal.

operators were eager to get into the business. One of them was a southerner, Thomas Gibbons, whose operation of a passenger steamboat between Elizabeth, New Jersey and Manhattan in brazen defiance of the Livingston interests led to a final decision against the monopoly in the U.S. Supreme Court. Gibbons had a talent for hiring the right man for the right job. The lawyer he engaged to argue his case in the Supreme Court was Daniel Webster. The skipper he employed to make the initial illegal runs between New Jersey and New York—and to stay one step ahead of the law while doing so—was a young Staten Island Dutchman who had already made a few dollars of his own ferrying passengers and cargo across New York Harbor under sail. His name was Cornelius Vanderbilt.

Everyone knows "Commodore" Vanderbilt the railroad baron, master of the New York Central and progenitor of one of the great American fortunes, but long before Vanderbilt took up with trains he was "Cornele the Boatman." From the waters off Staten Island (where he was born in 1794), Cornele graduated to Gibbons' service, and soon to proprietorship of his own line of Hudson River steamers—the "People's Line." He was operating packets on Long Island Sound when he got the name "Commodore," and from there he went on to transatlantic ventures. Had he stuck to steamships, he would have been a very rich man—but it was a different sort of business, centered in the Hudson Valley, that would make him the richest man in the United States.

Vanderbilt thought little of railroads at first, disparaging them as "them things that go on land." But by the 1850s, directorships on a number of roads convinced him that it was time to refocus his energies and his capital. In 1864, when he was already 70 years old, he sold his ships and put his money into railroads. His first acquisition was the New York and Harlem, a generally disregarded route that meandered too far east of the Hudson River on its way to a terminus opposite Albany. Vanderbilt didn't care where the tracks went; he bought the property because it came with access rights into downtown Manhattan. The Commodore used these to his advantage when he bought the Hudson River Railroad, with its "water-level" route laid directly along the east bank of the river. He now controlled the most direct route between New York City and the upriver docks that received freight from Albany.

CHRIS MAYNARD PHOTOS BOTH PAGES

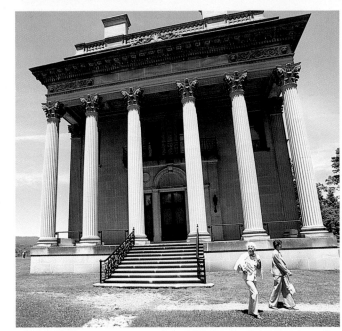

Above: The modern version of one machine that changed Hudson River travel.
Left: On the grounds of the Vanderbilt mansion.

The rails connecting with western New York State were owned by the New York Central, which hurt Vanderbilt's business by sending freight downriver in summer on steamboats rather than on the Commodore's road. The old veteran of the Livingston wars fought back by denying the Central a freight connection in winter. The Central knuckled under, and two years later its stockholders asked Vanderbilt to take control of the road. He now had complete mastery over trackage between New York and Buffalo, and by 1868 would begin the financial maneuverings that extended his New York Central system to Chicago before his death in 1877. But regardless of his later triumphs, it was the Commodore's success in commanding the routes that paralleled the Hudson and linked Albany with the hinterlands that put him in the first rank of American railroad entrepreneurs. His was a Hudson River fortune, at base, and it was far greater than those of the proud patroons who shared his Dutch ancestry. The arrow-straight mainline that follows the east shore of the Hudson belongs to Conrail today, but every train that rushes beneath the Highlands (and beneath the Hyde Park mansion built by Cornelius's grandson, Frederick Vanderbilt) is in a sense a reminder of the Commodore's genius in consolidating his water-level route, and of the Hudson Valley's continuing vitality as a great avenue of transport.

The Valley matures as an economic power

Just as the canals and steamships revolutionized travel in their day, so too did the railroads change the face of the Hudson Valley's economic life in the latter part of the 19th century. Within a matter of decades the canals, touted in the 1820s as a revolutionary means of conquering distance, seemed quaint and outmoded; steamboats, too, would feel the competitive power of "them things that go on land," and the old trading sloops would fade into history. Towns and cities that had arrived on the map because of their importance as river ports turned their attention instead to the tracks of the New York Central on the Delaware and Hudson rivers, and a new era of industry and trade began to build upon the formidable accomplishments of the first half of the 19th century. By 1850, New York State produced nearly a quarter of all the nation's manufactured goods, and along with New York City the communities of the Hudson Valley accounted for the lion's share of that output.

Some industries flourished in particular areas because of the nearness of vital natural resources. Albany, for instance, stood at the ideal location for receiving the timber wealth of the Adirondacks and turning it into paper and building materials. In the early 1870s, its mills were shipping well over half a billion board feet of lumber each year. The capital city also benefitted from the discovery of iron ore deposits in New York State; over a century ago, before the rise of the midwestern foundries, one in six Albany area workers was engaged in the stove industry. Flour milling, too, was important to Albany before cities like Buffalo and Minneapolis began processing closer to the grain belt.

Troy was also a great foundry city, specializing in components for railroad cars and in rail itself, but its real triumph was in textiles. Long before the South began to mill the cotton it grew, Troy boasted New York State's first facility

Above: Bridges at Poughkeepsie.

Facing page: Corn and autumn color near Prattsville.
JIM CRONK

27

In downtown Catskill.

Northeast. The word steps vividly out of socio-economic jargon and into the realm of the hard and tangible when you stand beside a piece of work like the abandoned steel railroad bridge at Poughkeepsie. It takes a straight leap across half the city in order to achieve the altitude it needs to span the Hudson far above the largest ships, and is probably the biggest single unused object in the valley if not the entire Northeast. But to dwell upon the melancholy bridge is to neglect the impact of a postindustrial institution such as International Business Machines, which has an enormous facility in Poughkeepsie and numerous others throughout the lower Hudson Valley. The river cities often look down but they are not out. There is life after heavy manu-facturing.

Agriculture and tourism

Agriculture in the Hudson Valley is largely concentrated along the east shore of the river. It wasn't until the mid-19th century that the perquisites of feudalism were finally legislated out of existence, after many an anti-rent uprising on the part of the small leaseholders. Men like the Livingstons and van Rensselaers had not supported the American cause in the revolution out of radical economic sympathies, but because they wanted independence from the taxing authority of Britain. But the 20th century has posed challenges of an entirely new sort to Hudson Valley farmers. The story is familiar to their counterparts in nearby Connecticut: as the cities push out into their older suburbs, rural areas become suburbanized. In the past, the pioneers of the exurban land rush were merely a handful of mansion-building magnificoes from New York City, and they concentrated their estates along the Hudson. But nowadays the bedroom communities of the middle class have multiplied beyond Westchester, north into Putnam and Dutchess counties. The process is accelerated by the decentralization of high-tech manufacturing; today you may not have to commute as far as Manhattan but only into Poughkeepsie or Kingston. Land is simply becoming too valuable for farmers to say no to subdividers. The old rural character of the eastern Hudson Valley survives best from Rhinebeck and Amenia north, especially in the areas that hug the Massachusetts and Connecticut borders, and is least changed north and east of Troy, where the country-side blends imperceptibly into the rolling dairyland of Vermont.

Tourism is an old business along the Hudson Valley and in the Catskills, no doubt dating back to the first time someone

for processing the fiber from bales to finished products. When a man bought a shirt a century ago, there was a good chance it was made in Troy. Smaller Hudson Valley cities such as Kingston, Hudson, Poughkeepsie and Newburgh also developed thriving clothing industries.

The era in which the primary resource industries loomed large in the Hudson Valley generally lasted only until the Civil War. Afterwards, as new resource-rich areas to the west were opened up, the cluster of older cities in New York's oldest quarter turned more to specialty manufactures and the production of consumer goods. Well into the 20th century, the Hudson Valley was the world's largest producer of common brick. Albany made billiard balls, millions of them; Troy made sandpaper; Yonkers became a world capital of the elevator industry. The progression is common to most, if not all, developed areas and leads in turn to a decline in industrial production generally as manufacturing plants age and proprietors turn to less expensive labor markets. The ugly term "rustbelt" was coined, in large part, to describe communities such as those in the Hudson Valley left to fend for themselves following the postwar ebb of industrial affluence in the took a sloop upriver simply to look at the Palisades and the Highlands rather than to trade or explore. The northern, more easterly portion of the Catskill range is one of America's oldest resort areas; the first hotels catering to summer guests were built early in the 19th century. (The southwestern Catskills, of mega-resort and "Borscht Belt" fame, were developed considerably later.) Saratoga Springs, near the head of the valley proper, was a favored retreat even of the Indians, who knew of the mineral waters and had faith in their restorative powers. By the middle of the last century, "taking the waters" was a popular excuse for a fashionable vacation, although—as to this day—a majority of visitors spent more time at the racetrack than at the spa.

And there is the river itself, the Hudson as a pathway through its magnificent valley. "The most charming inland water trip on the American continent," boasted an 1882 circular for the Hudson River Day Line in the typically hyperbolic advertising prose of the day—but in this case, we need not take the claim with a grain of salt. If we discount the wilderness rivers upon which travel is an adventure rather than a stately progression, it's doubtful that we could come up with a more beautiful waterway. Small wonder that excursion steamers followed almost immediately on the heals of Robert Fulton's "invention," or that public and private pleasure craft still ply the river regardless of what environmental chemists might have to say about its water. There is something about following the broad channel northward, past the lordly Palisades and between the steep, forested Highlands as they crowd down upon the gorge beyond the Tappan Zee—something promising and portentous, as if the river were still an avenue of access to a prize even more wonderful than Henry Hudson's dreamed-of Cathay. It flows forward and backward in time, the Hudson does, just as it flows in two compass directions in fulfillment of Algonquin prophecies. Measured in the days and years of civilization it is the oldest big river in the United States; it was our St. Lawrence and our Rhine when the Mississippi was still a wild Amazon.

Left: Workout time at Sarasota Springs.
Below: Saratoga Battlefield, where patriot victories in September and October 1777 convinced the French to join the fight against the British.

THE UPPER VALLEY: THE RIVER ABOVE ALBANY

This view from the American position at the Saratoga battlefield shows how the patriot forces commanded the Hudson.

CHRIS MAYNARD PHOTOS BOTH PAGES

The source of the Hudson River is a little pond in the Adirondacks, much closer to Montreal than to New York City. Lake Tear in the Clouds fills a tiny glacial pocket on the shoulder of Mt. Marcy. The 5,344' peak that the Indians called Tahawas, "cloud-splitter," is the highest mountain in New York State. Such origins possess the symmetry of myth—the state's highest mountain, its greatest river—but none of the Hudson's eventual character is revealed in its uppermost reaches. For the first wilderness miles the stream is not even called the Hudson. It's the Opalescent River, a name that clearly has to change if we are to imagine Albany on its banks and Manhattan at its mouth. The Opalescent becomes the Hudson after it receives the flow from a secondary source in Henderson and Sanford lakes, and joins a clutch of western tributaries near the town of Newcomb.

Route 28N is the last of civilization that the Hudson sees for another 30 miles as it gains depth and force, along its boulder-strewn channel, from the waters of the Goodnow, the Rock, the Indian and the Boreas rivers, cold mountain streams all. North River and North Creek, once logging centers now catering largely to skiers and summer vacationers, are the next towns along the Hudson; the name Sodom, stuck to a small town on a tributary just south of North Creek, doubtless refers back to the fleshpots of lumberjack days and not to modern apres-ski shenanigans. They don't name towns quite so frankly anymore. North Creek, incidentally, is where Theodore Roosevelt began the first leg of the rail journey that took him to Buffalo and his oath of office as President. He had been camping at Mt. Marcy—ever the practitioner as

Pulp logs at Glens Falls.

well as the proselytizer of the "strenuous life"—when word reached him that President McKinley's condition had taken a turn for the worse a week after he had been shot by an

31

anarchist at a Buffalo exposition. T.R., who had already been to Buffalo where he was told McKinley would likely recover, began his hasty second journey by horse and wagon. He took no time to pack, and was probably the first man to be sworn in as president wearing borrowed clothes.

Near Warrensburg, a scant seven miles west of Lake George, the Hudson meets the first of its major tributaries, the Schroon River flowing south out of Schroon Lake. The confluence of the two streams marks the northernmost focal point of the Hudson's economic history: it was here, in the spring of the year when Adirondack meltwater made the river high and fast, that the great 19th-century log drivers of the Hudson and the Schroon were merged. The logs then thundered south, past the outlet of Great Sacandaga Lake at Hadley, past Corinth and east into the hungry mills of Glens Falls.

Glens Falls: Fortunes in paper, a fortune in art

At Glens Falls the Hudson is no longer a mountain stream but a broad, working river, spectacularly punctuated by a 60-foot waterfall. The falls were the reason this place became the terminus of the great log drives, as they provided the power for the earliest lumber mills. "Glen's Falls," they were called, after Col. John Glen of Schenectady built the first mills in 1788; eight years before, the little town that straddled the river had been leveled by the British during one of their sorties of the upper valley. Before that the area was part of the "Queensbury Patent," an enormous land grant whose name is recalled in the name of Glens Falls' present-day Queensbury Hotel.

The timber wealth of the Adirondacks poured into Glens Falls throughout the 19th century, its flow accelerated by the intensity of logging and by great leaps in literacy and printing technology. Just before the turn of the century, the city's factories were producing 275 tons of paper each day. Although labor troubles in the early 1900s and diversification into other manufactures in later years have diminished the role of pulp and paper in Glens Falls' economy, the industry remains an important one.

Among the many fine mansions the paper business made possible in the wealthy precincts of Glens Falls, the best known today is a Florentine-inspired villa built in 1912 by Louis and Charlotte Pruyn Hyde. Mrs. Hyde was an heiress to the Finch, Pruyn and Company paper fortune, and her husband was a Boston lawyer. Their passion was collecting art. They built their house as a showplace for their acquisitions and early on decided that someday it should be open to the public. Throughout the rest of her life (Louis Hyde died in 1934), Charlotte Pruyn Hyde expanded her collection, buying with an eye for quality not always evident in someone with such eclectic taste. Her purchases included works by Turner, Rembrandt, Fragonard, Rubens and Van Dyck, as well as Homer, Eakins, Whistler, Picasso and Matisse. Having determined that her house should open as a museum after her death, she had plenty of time to get it in order: she passed away in 1963, when she was 96 years old. Since then, visitors to Glens Falls have been able to browse through more than four centuries of art of the western world in an intimate private *palazzo* built in the twilight of America's gilded age. Officially called the Hyde Collection, it's all testimony to what paper money can buy, on Warren Avenue right in Glens Falls.

A link with Lake Champlain

At Glens Falls the Hudson takes a turn due east and then shifts sharply to the south. Here are the small twin cities of Hudson Falls and Fort Edward, both traditionally paper-making centers but now better known as the site of a huge General Electric manufacturing plant. To the Indians, Fort Edward was *Wahcoloosencoochaleva*, the "Great Carrying Place" that marked the southern end of the long portage from Lake Champlain and Lake George. Using this carry across the height of land that separates the Champlain and Hudson drainage basins, it would be possible to canoe from the Gulf of St. Lawrence to New York harbor, by way of the St. Lawrence River, the Richelieu River, Lake Champlain and the Hudson, but since 1822 the hardships of portage have not been necessary. In that year the Champlain Canal was opened between the southern tip of the lake, near Whitehall, and the Hudson at Fort Edward. Complete two years before the famed Erie Canal, the 25-mile Champlain link remains in use today—primarily by recreational craft, but occasionally by commercial barges as well. It is odd to come across a relic of the days before the railroads and highways, still functioning after so many other canals have gone to ruin, but the modernized Champlain is kept in good order by the New York Department of Transportation. A good place to see it is near the intersection of Routes 22 and 4 in Comstock, where Lock No. 11 assists northbound vessels with a 12-foot lift, from 112 to 124 feet above sea level.

Above: The Great Meadow Corrections Facility near Comstock. *Facing page, top:* Lock C-2 on the Champlain Canal at Waterford. *Bottom:* At Lock 11, Champlain Canal at Comstock.

Within sight of the canal at Comstock are the razor-wired fences and guard towers of the Great Meadow Corrections Facility, an incongruous presence amidst the slate hills and dairy farms of the border country. On the one side the prison, on the other the placid little canal piecing together the vast water route between Quebec and New York City—symbols of confinement and freedom, accidentally juxtaposed.

A revolutionary hero, a literary grandfather

If you cross the Hudson at Fort Edward and follow Route 32 down toward Saratoga Springs, the first town you come to is Gansevoort, little more than a country crossroads. Here is an ancient white mansion that was the provincial seat of a legendary Dutch squire and hero of the Revolution, Gen. Peter Gansevoort. In July of 1776, just as independence was declared, Gansevoort, a colonel then, took command of Fort George on Lake George; a year later, he was charged with the defense of Fort Stanwix (later Fort Schuyler), at the Mohawk Valley site where the city of Rome now stands. In August of 1777, Gansevoort and his garrison of 550 men held off a three-week siege laid by nearly three times as many British, Tory and Indian attackers under Col. Barry St. Leger, thus

33

Horse racing, gamblimg and "The Waters" made Sarasota Springs' fortune.

Wooden "redcoats" greet visitors at today's Saratoga Springs.

bringing to a halt the western prong of the three-part British move to isolate New England from New York. "It is my determined resolution," Gansevoort replied to St. Leger's demand for surrender, "to defend this fort at every hazard, to the last extremity, in behalf of the United American States, who have placed me here to defend it against all their enemies."

In 1783, the year peace between Great Britain and her former colonies was proclaimed, Gen. Gansevoort took title to the land surrounding the mansion, which would eventually bear his family name. Here the old warrior—a giant in those days at six feet four—lived until his death in 1812. The legend in which he basked during those years as a country squire would have assured his place in history even if his daughter

Maria hadn't married a New York importer named Allan Melville, by whom she had a son named Herman.

Herman Melville named one of his own sons Stanwix.

Saratoga: spa and battlefield

The most famous single place name in the Hudson Valley north of Albany is undoubtedly Saratoga. Already celebrated as the site of a watershed battle of the American Revolution, Saratoga in the mid-19th century became something this nation had never had before—a national resort, part Newport and part Las Vegas, with the accent on the exclusivity of the former and the raffishness of the latter. The blanket use of the name "Saratoga," has caused some confusion, however: the place where the battle was fought, now a national historic park, is not the site of the spa near which the city of Saratoga Springs grew. About 10 miles separate the two. The battlefield is on the Hudson, while the spa and city lie to the west.

Legend has it that the first white visitor to Saratoga was Sir William Johnson, American hero of the Battle of Lake George in the French and Indian War. Johnson took a French musket ball in the leg during the battle, and eight years later he still was not fully recovered. Some Mohawk friends brought him to their healing springs, and while we can't be sure what the outcome was for Johnson, we do know that by the time of the Revolution at least one inn was catering to those who came to drink or bathe in the waters. The town began to grow in the days immediately after the war, and within 50 years rows of wooden hotels lined the streets. By the time America was enjoying the years of post-Civil War prosperity that Mark Twain labeled the "Gilded Age," Saratoga could boast the largest hotel in the world—the six-story, 917-room Grand Union. On the verandas of the Grand Union and other elaborate hostelries, pomaded swells and bustle-skirted women were the stars of their own lavish spectacle. One conspicuous fop set an all-time record of more than 40 changes of clothes in one day.

"The Waters" remained the ostensible purpose for being there. The waters of Saratoga come bubbling out of the ground from dozens of different apertures, some still in their natural state and some long since capped with spigots and fountains. The springs' mineral content varies from site to site; some are saline, some alkaline, some both. Their mineral traces, along with natural carbonation, are what give the waters their reputation as an elixir (some springs do offer a powerful physic) and a medium

Top, left and right: *Equine stars of Saratoga Springs.*
Left: *The Schuyler House in Saratoga Springs.*

for bathing. The baths were one popular means of "taking the waters," in between changes of clothes, and another was a visit to the "Hall of Springs" where visitors could imbibe their choice of offerings from the bizarre local water table.

But water alone does not a resort make. Saratoga Springs became a horse racing capital, where stables financed by America's greatest fortunes vied for glory on the flat and harness tracks, and—back when such things were legal in New York State—a casino gambling mecca. Racing continues to thrive in Saratoga, with thoroughbreds competing on the flat track during July and August and trotters running in harness from April until November. Saratoga Springs even has a National Museum of Racing, exhibiting oil portraits of famous horses and a colorful collection of hundreds of racing silks. As for the gaming tables, they have not been permitted in New York for more than 75 years, although the wide open days of blackjack and faro at Saratoga Springs are recalled in The Casino, a restored Victorian gambling house set in downtown Congress Park.

Above: The 155' Saratoga Battlefield monument honors three of the four victorious American generals in the battle. An empty niche denotes the later treachery of Gen. Benedict Arnold.
Right: Peaceful farms across the Hudson from the Saratoga Battlefield.
Facing page: Detail from the Saratoga Monument.

The waters may no longer be taken as seriously as they once were in Saratoga, but they are still taken. The state of New York has owned the rights to the mineral springs since 1910, and today they join a theater, golf course and summer performing arts center as focal points of an expansive state park. If you want to play at being a pampered gilded-age captain of finance (or even if you just want to get rid of a few minor aches and pains), by all means head to the Roosevelt baths for a long, private soak in effervescent mineral water, brought precisely to body temperature, and a professional massage. This is state government working as it should. While you lie half-somnolent in the tub, you can think about how

many outfits you are going to wear during the evening, or perhaps how to finagle the Commodore out of some Erie stock.

Saratoga Springs today is several shades more democratic in character than it was a hundred years ago. Except for the Adelphi with its graceful columns and Eastlake lobby furniture, and the solid old Rip Van Dam (a Hudson Valley name if there ever was one), the legendary downtown hotels have been replaced by a string of motels out on Route 9—one of which presumptuously calls itself the Grand Union. But the downtown streets are still worth wandering for their shops and restaurants: two favorite destinations are a first-rate pastry shop called Bocca Dolce, on Phila Street; and the nearby Caffe Lena, an early 1960s period piece said to be the oldest continuously operated coffee house in the country. Don McLean, of "American Pie" fame, got his start there, and it is still a busy stop on the folksinging circuit.

Standing in marked contrast to busy, gregarious Saratoga Springs are the melancholy hills along the Hudson where the Battle of Saratoga was fought. Like so many of history's great killing grounds, the land encompassed within the national park is now empty and quiet. Only the markers along the tour road, and the cannon placed as they were on those early autumn days in 1777, are reminders of the desperate struggle that ruined the season's harvest and turned the tide of the American Revolution. On Bemis Heights, where Continental officers billeted at the Nielson Farm, the surrounding fields roll toward the river in the stillness of a haunted place.

Saratoga was a two-part battle. On September 19, 1777, Gen. John Burgoyne advanced upon the American positions on the heights above the Hudson at Stillwater. He had some 9,000 men, nearly half of them British and the rest mostly German mercenaries, along with a few hundred Canadians and Indians. American artillery commanded the river road, forcing Burgoyne to move his troops through the forest in order to attack the redoubts designed for the Americans by Col. Thaddeus Kosciusko. American small-arms fire held the day against British bayonet charges, and a total rout of the attackers might have been possible if German reinforcements had not arrived in time. With the battle ending in virtual stalemate, both sides retrenched and waited.

Nearly three weeks passed. No reinforcements came to help the British, while the American ranks under Gen. Horatio Gates swelled with 4,000 fresh militiamen. Finally, on the seventh of October, Burgoyne made his move. In one day's furious fighting, he lost more than 400 of his officers and men and all eight of his advance cannons, as three columns of American troops overwhelmed his right and left flanks, and an attack led by Benedict Arnold routed the Germans who held the center redoubts. On the next day, October 8, Burgoyne began his northward retreat. His broken army was run to ground nine days later at Saratoga, surrounded by 20,000 Continental troops. With Burgoyne's surrender on October 17, the grand British strategy to dominate the Hudson Valley was permanently undone.

In the countryside just north of Saratoga National Park stands an ornate 155-foot obelisk, the Saratoga monument. Its observation level has been off limits since 1987 because of unsafe stairs, but the arched niches above its base still tell a sad story. Set into three of the niches are statues of Gens. Schuyler and Gates and Col. Horatio Morgan, heroes all at Saratoga. The fourth niche is empty, reminding us that another hero of the battle, Gen. Benedict Arnold, cannot be honored here or anywhere else this side of the Atlantic.

THE CAPITAL DISTRICT

3

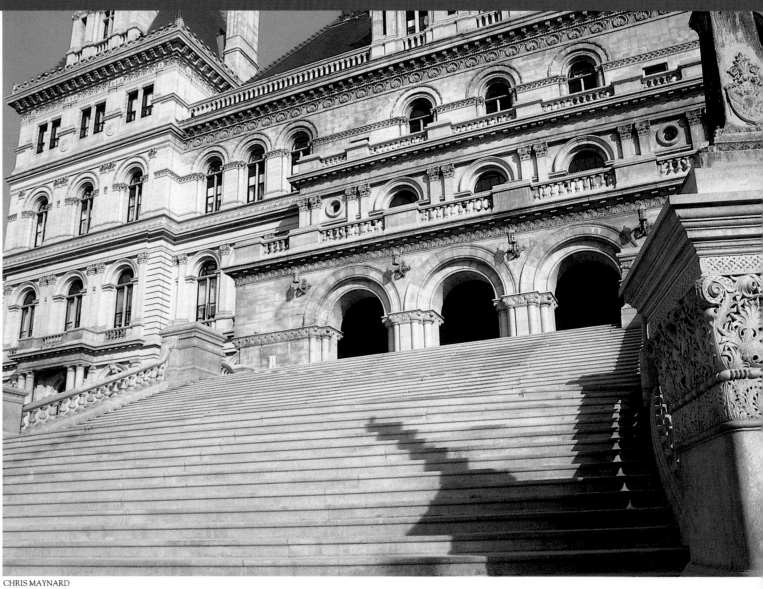

The Empire State's Capitol in Albany.

CHRIS MAYNARD

The cities of Albany and Troy make up the first great urban concentration encountered by the Hudson on its southward path to the sea.

Of course, rivers do not simply happen upon important cities; they create them. The creation of what was to become New York's capital district and the seat of much of its upstate industry began very early in the history of European settlement of the valley—at the beginning, really, when the rough palisades of Fort Nassau were raised on Castle Island just five years after Henry Hudson coaxed his *Half Moon* to the natural head of navigation for large vessels on the Hudson. The development of the inland towns proceeded as the growth of commerce on the river proceeded, and accelerated tremendously when canals and, later, railroads made Albany a lucrative way station rather than merely a northern terminus for high-volume shipping. The area's biggest business, the governing of what was for most of America's history the richest and most populous state in the union, was a natural if not inevitable outgrowth of this commercial ascendancy. Plenty of states and nations allow the management of politics to devolve by default upon their largest cities; New York as state capital would have made conventional sense. But the burghers of Albany were powerful enough to win the presence of the governor and legislature as early as 1797 (Kingston and Poughkeepsie had been interim stops, after New York's hold had been weakened by years of British occupation during the war), and since that year the two cities, one a state capital and the other a world power, have maintained a dynamic tension from their opposite ends of the valley. New York constantly reminds Albany that it is managing the affairs of more than a minor province, and Albany reminds New York that it is tied to the destiny of smaller towns and cities that helped make it rich in the days of the Erie Canal and the New York Central railroad. Albany—in particular its governor's mansion—is the place to which New York Mayor Edward Koch could not move, once he had pronounced upstate life ridiculous.

The real history of Albany began with the building of Fort Orange in 1624. Named by the Dutch in honor of their ruling House of Orange, the settlement was first occupied by 18 families of Walloon refugees from what is now part of Belgium. But in its earliest years, Fort Orange was less a magnet for permanent homesteading that a staging area for the fur trade: in 1636, the community's trappers killed 30,000 beaver and shipped the pelts down the Hudson and, as late as 1643, it harbored only a hundred or so settlers, living in what the Jesuit missionary Isaac Jogues recorded as 25 or 30 houses scattered along the riverbank.

During the third and fourth decades of the 17th century the peopling and provisioning of the Fort Orange vicinity was undertaken more strenuously by the van Rensselaer patroonship than by the Dutch West India Company. Kiliaen van Rensselaer and his agents established their domain on both sides of the Hudson south of the Mohawk and brought in settlers from Scotland, Germany and the Scandinavian countries as well as from the Netherlands. The patroon built sawmills and cleared farms, and the newcomers paid him the rent mandated by his position. It was perhaps inevitable that

Above: In Albany.
Right: The Capitol.

the West India Company and the patroon should clash over land rights at Fort Orange. The controversy came to a head in 1652, when Peter Stuyvesant, who managed the company's affairs from his downriver headquarters at New Amsterdam, proclaimed the area around the fort independent of Rensselaerswyck. He called the new town Beverwyck (bever being Dutch for "beaver"), and set up the Company's own court to handle its affairs. The van Rensselaer interests never recognized Beverwyck's independence from the patroonship, and spited Stuyvesant by refusing him assistance when the English came to seize New Amsterdam in 1664. Even under the new regime, van Rensselaer claimed what is now Albany (after the Duke of York and Albany) as part of his fiefdom. The claim was finally renounced in 1685, and the following year Albany was granted its city charter by the colonial government of New York.

Albany Comes of Age

Along with its city charter, Albany was granted an immensely lucrative fur-trading monopoly. The royal decree conferred upon the city exclusive rights to the commerce in beaver pelts "to the eastward, northward, and westward as far as His Majesty's dominion may extend." In practical terms this meant that Albany's trapping privileges reached throughout the Adirondacks, and east and west into the Champlain and Mohawk valleys—all of this in an area laced with streams and teeming with beaver. The only real limit on the whole vast prize was the extent of the French hegemony, ever threatening to extend southward beyond the St. Lawrence Valley. As we noted earlier, Albany's situation was a delicate one throughout the remainder of the years in which France and Britain continued to face each other down along the indefinite border of Canada and the English colonies. On the one hand New France was an impediment; on the other, Montreal was such a valuable commercial partner that New England sometimes wondered just where the Albany traders' allegiance lay. In the end, of course, the city proved to be a bulwark of British power in the French and Indian Wars.

One of the heroes of that conflict, and later an even more important figure in the American Revolution, was a scion of Dutch settlers named Philip Schuyler. Schuyler's gracious Georgian mansion on Albany's Catherine Street is perhaps the city's greatest tangible reminder of the late colonial era, when its safety was finally assured and its century of dominance as a great inland port was about to begin. The house was built to its owner's design early in the 1760s, when this part of Albany made up Schuyler's 125-acre estate. After its owner was invested by the Continental Congress with the title of major general and charged with the colonies' northern defenses, the house became his headquarters; here General John Burgoyne and his staff were held prisoner after the British debacle at Saratoga. (Schuyler, as it happened, had fallen afoul of the politicians and had been removed from command during the battle.) Three years later, in 1780, Gen. Schuyler gave his daughter Elizabeth's hand in marriage to Alexander Hamilton in a downstairs drawing room. Schuyler, later a New York senator, lived in his Albany house until his death in 1804 (the same year in which his illustrious son-in-law was killed in a duel by Aaron Burr). More than a century later, it was opened to the public as a museum.

By the time Gen. Schuyler was parlaying his military fame into a career as a Federalist politician in the 1790s, the tenor of Albany life that had created him and his Dutch patrician class had already begun to change. To the Yankee entrepreneurs who began to flood into Albany in the 1790s and early 1800s, the fur trade was an anachronism, and a century and a half of proper Dutch lineage was no requisite for prominence and prosperity. Albany was now the capital of New York, and, more important, it was the capital of inland commerce in the Northeast. If a New England farmer wanted to move his family to the fertile new lands of western New York or Ohio he passed through Albany; if he wanted to ship his grain crops back east to market once he settled, he shipped them through Albany. Even before the canals and steamboats revolutionized commerce along the Hudson Valley and in western New York, Albany was a vital crossroads. Hundreds of west-moving wagons were stocked with provisions here, and in the years around 1800 nearly two dozen stagecoaches left Albany each day to clatter over the turnpike that paralleled the modern-day U.S. Route 20 south of the Mohawk River. The quays of north Albany were heaped with Adirondack lumber (the city would eventually become the world's third largest shipper of white pine) and salt from the mines near Syracuse. The upstate glass business had begun to prosper, and its wares, too, sought markets by way of Albany. The opening of the Erie Canal sent this mercantile economy into high gear: between 1820 and 1830,

In 1685, Albany recived its city charter from the government of New York colony.

Albany City Hall.

the population of Albany doubled. By 1831, 15,000 canal boats called at the great inland port. Ocean-going sailing vessels, too, tied up at Albany's docks—some 500 in that same year of 1831. The forest of masts along city wharves must have stirred the imagination of a 12-year-old boy named Herman Melville, who had moved with his family from New York City to Albany two years before. In 1832 his father died, and as his prospects diminished with his mother's impoverishment—despite the local prominence of her Gansevoort maiden name—the young Herman Melville coming of age in Albany and nearby Lansingburgh must have

Stained glass in the New York State Capitol.

expansive period that he grew to young manhood and set out on his first great adventure. His novel *Redburn* is the fictionalized story of that voyage, and it begins quite properly in Albany.

Albany the political capital

The litany of Albany's commercial and industrial accomplishments in the 19th century reads like the story of the trajectory of so many other northeastern cities—there was Albany the cattle town, situated so perfectly at the backdoor of the hungry metropolis that 2 million head passed through its stockyards each year; Albany the foundry; and of course Albany the upstate linchpin in Commodore Vanderbilt's New York Central empire. But while all of these roles were in the making, Albany was practicing for its greatest and most public accomplishments, as a center of American politics exceeded in power and flamboyance only by the national capital itself.

As the state of New York in the early 1800s began to eclipse the old New England ports in terms of commercial prowess, so too did its politicians rise in influence. During the 1820s, 1830s and 1840s, the prevailing power in New York State politics was the "Albany Regency," a loose coalition of Democratic Party officials and theoreticians. One of their number, Martin Van Buren, served briefly as governor of New York and later as secretary of state and vice president in Andrew Jackson's administration before being elected president himself in 1836. (Van Buren was the first of four men to occupy the governor's mansion in Albany before going on to the White House; the others were Grover Cleveland, Theodore Roosevelt and Franklin D. Roosevelt.) Another powerful voice in the Albany Regency, Thurlow Weed, edited the city's *Evening Journal* from 1830 to 1865 and eventually became one of the original boosters of the Republican Party.

As the century progressed and the great railroad fortunes burgeoned, politics in Albany was not always conducted in the best traditions of democratic altruism. Plenty of stories exist of rail barons' agents heading upriver from New York with the wherewithal to purchase favorable legislation and court decisions—sometimes, in fact, the prime movers showed up themselves. The story is told of how Jay Gould, the most notorious finagler of the Gilded Age, traveled to Albany with a satchel of cash, allegedly half a million dollars, that he used to bribe the state Senate into legalizing a vastly inflated issue of Erie Railroad stock that he and his accomplices had foisted off on

felt a growing inevitability about those docks and those ships. When he was 17, he took a boat to New York and from there shipped out on a merchantman bound for England. We alternatively think of Melville as a product of New York City where he was born and where he died, or as a New England author. But it was in Albany at the beginning of its most

Cornelius Vanderbilt. The Commodore's men had already been to the capital, spreading money around in pursuit of the opposite goal. But Gould won the prize for absolute cheek: while he was making the rounds of legislative offices like a black-bearded Santa Claus, he was ostensibly locked in his hotel under a sheriff's custody, pursuant to a Vanderbilt-rigged court injunction. No doubt the sheriff got his, too; it was a grand time to be alive and shamelessly corrupt.

Albany politicians of that same Gilded Age built themselves the most extravagant seat of government ever conceived for an American state capital—that is, until Nelson Rockefeller worked out his own dreams in marble just across the street, a hundred years later. The State Capitol at Albany was the most expensive building ever constructed in the United States at the time it was dedicated. It had consumed 25 million gold-standard dollars, 32 years of labor and the services of four architects. To this day, there is no more impressive place to visit in Albany.

The State Capitol is unusual for a truly fine building in that it represents a polyglot of architectural styles, indicative of its three decades of construction and four principal designers. If the eye begins to take in the structure from the ground up (no mean feat, as it covers three acres), the initial impression of the first three storeys is of a French Second Empire design akin, say, to the old State Department (now the Executive Office Building) in Washington, D.C. This was the plan of the original architect, Thomas Fuller, when he accepted the commission in 1868 (preliminary construction had begun the year before). Beginning at the fourth floor, however, the style of the Capitol turns decidedly Romanesque. This is the influence of the great Henry Hobson Richardson, who with Leopold Eidlitz replaced Fuller in 1876. And the roof, with its red tile corner peaks and steep, gray-slated central mass, suggests the chateaux of the French Renaissance. Somehow it all works wonderfully, a grand looting of styles for the imperial palace of the Empire State.

The Capitol's interior is no less eclectic, and no less impressive, than its granite outer walls. Exquisite wood paneling and stone-carving are everywhere. Richardson's hand is strongly evident, particularly in the marble-walled senate chamber, with a pair of fireplaces worthy of Citizen Kane; and the Great Western or "Million Dollar" Staircase, a fantastic brownstone construction decorated by dozens of

JIM CRONK

The New York State Capitol was the most expensive building in the U.S. at the time of its dedication in 1899.

stonecarvers with likenesses of famous New Yorkers as well as friends and families of the carvers themselves. The Executive Chamber, also the work of Richardson, is a vast oaken salon that looks more like the haunt of a Renaissance doge than a popularly elected chief executive of an American state. Official New York was in exuberant spirits when it set up this vast pile. It announced that however lavish the stone pronunciamentos of the moguls who stood astride the harbor to the south, the city at the head of the broad Hudson would be suitably castled as well.

In 1899, Gov. Theodore Roosevelt declared the place finished at last. It certainly suited his requirements for a backdrop—he could, and did, bound up the 77 Capitol steps two at a time, and project a presence big enough to fill that paneled cavern of an Executive Chamber. Thirty years later his distant cousin would likewise pull those chamber walls close around him, and he did it from a wheelchair.

Henry Hobson Richardson, who ironically enough did not like Albany and resented every night he had to spend there while at work on his commissions, gave the city one other great monument. This is the 1882 City Hall, executed in the bluff, massive, yet richly textured style with which the

Enjoying the Hudson in winter.

43

Above and facing page: Nelson Rockefeller's Empire State Plaza, which took 16 years to build.

architect's name is alliteratively associated: Richardson Romanesque. The building's great stone tower houses a 60-bell carillon, a lightsome touch in a building of such ponderousness and weight.

Perhaps the most remarkable thing about Albany's City Hall is that for more than four of its first 10 decades, its chief office was occupied by one man. This was the late Erastus Corning, scion of an old Albany family (an earlier Erastus Corning was the first president of the New York Central Railroad in the days before it became Cornelius Vanderbilt's prize) who took office as mayor on January 1, 1942 and held on, through 11 consecutive terms, until his death in the spring of 1983. Corning owed his longevity as mayor not only to his own winning personality and political sense, but to the perpetual backing of one Daniel Peter O'Connell, head of the Albany County Democratic Party and master of a machine that was the equal of Hague's in New Jersey, Curley's in Boston or even Daley's in Chicago. O'Connell ran the local

party—and by extension, the city—from the early 1920s until his death, at 91, in 1977. In his fine profile and reminiscence of his native city titled *O Albany!*, novelist William Kennedy calculated that in order to have voted for any Democrat for mayor of Albany other than one of O'Connell's hand-picked candidates, a resident of the city would have to have been 79 years old at the time of the boss's death. The momentum of the old man's repeated anointments of Erastus Corning—and, to be fair, Corning's own savvy—kept the mayor-for-life in office for another two terms after O'Connell's death and secured him the successorship to party leadership as well. O'Connell and Corning, Irish saloonkeeper's son and Yankee patrician, were Albany politics throughout much of the 20th century.

But one other hand lay heavy on the city at midcentury and changed the skyline and downtown character of Albany with a drastic stroke unequalled in all the days since the building of Fort Orange. The hand was that of Gov. Nelson Rockefeller. His project—if such a pedestrian word can be used to define the object of a relationship akin to that of Louis XIV and Versailles—was the South Mall.

The South Mall, now officially the Gov. Nelson A. Rockefeller Empire State Plaza, is New York State's Brasilia, a capitol complex designed as a homogenous unit and built from scratch in the center of a drastically contrasting landscape. In this instance, though, the host landscape was not virgin forest but the worn 19th-century fabric of downtown Albany, specifically a 98-acre tract opposite the State Capitol. Eleven hundred and fifty buildings were demolished to make way for the mall, and more than 3,000 downtown residents relocated. It was proposed in 1962 and finished 16 years later.

Rockefeller built the Mall because the state needed office space. He built it the way he did because he wanted a monument to his taste, to his vision and to the way he thought the furniture should be arranged in the capital of a state that billed itself as an empire. The Mall is an immense, marble-clad platform, almost perfectly walled off from the city around it. Nine buildings rise chastely from the floor of the enclosure, as they never could from ordinary city streets. (Across Madison Avenue, a state museum stands on its own.) The Mall includes three low-rise buildings, one for the courts, one for the legislative offices and another nearly a quarter of a mile long housing state agencies; an ovoid theater known familiarly as the "Egg" although it is really only half of one, slashed lengthwise; four identical 23-storey office towers, and a 44-storey monolith, the Erastus Corning Tower,

anchoring the vast parcel on the south. All of the buildings are cloaked in the whitest marble; by some estimates, the project took the equivalent of three years' output of Vermont's quarries.

On the 42nd floor of the Corning Tower, there is an observation deck. It's worth a visit (the whole Mall is worth a visit, provided you find one of the entrances that penetrate its defenses, if only for the Disney World gargantuanism of it all), and on a clear day its views of the entire upper Hudson Valley and the Adirondack foothills are sublime. But the views of the Mall from the high ground across the river are no less fascinating. They put Rockefeller's monument in context, or

For more than a century, Troy was America's shirt and collar capital.

Farm near Troy.

decaying blocks came back to life when the project was finished and that it inspired private developers to launch bold new projects of their own. Perhaps. But the 1980s have been a time of downtown revitalization in cities across America, and more often than not the new life has been the result of the preservation and recycling of older structures, rather than the 1960s-style gutting of inner city streets and the building of megaprojects. Granted, the blighted rooming houses razed by Rockefeller were not golden-opportunity leftovers like Boston's Quincy Market or San Francisco's Ghirardelli chocolate factory, or even like Albany's own turn-of-the-century Union Station, which has been gloriously rehabbed by the Norstar Bank. Nevertheless, at least a good part of that 98-acre swath of the city could have survived like nearby Lark Street into the era of boutiques, chic bistros and renovated housing. There may be an air of yuppie triteness to these examples, but at least they have a street-scale texture missing from the attack of the marble megaliths.

Across the river to Troy

Just north of Albany on the opposite bank of the Hudson, the old city of Troy has been similarly struggling toward a downtown revival. Troy has had a more difficult row to hoe—it has no industry nearly as massive as the state government—and although it stands at the intersection of the Hudson with the New York State Barge Canal, its port cannot compare in size with that of Albany's, which was deepened to accommodate oceangoing shipping in the early 1930s.

Troy, which was settled on van Rensselaer lands as early as 1629 and incorporated as a village in 1798 (the classical name had been chosen to replace the more provincial "Vanderheyden" several years earlier), grew to boast an economy based at least as firmly in industry as in transportation. The arsenal in nearby Watervliet was an important employer from the time of the War of 1812, and experienced a tremendous boom during the Civil War. Early Trojan manufactures also included ironware such as bells, stoves and horseshoes, and the city's experience in building horse-drawn coaches eventually led to its involvement in the railroad car business. But one industry that remained dominant in Troy for well over a century actually had its birth here. It began in 1829, when a Trojan housewife named Hannah Lord Montague invented the man's detachable shirt collar. Within five years there were collar factories in Troy. Before long the city was a center of shirt manufacture as well, with mills expanding

rather they show how bizarrely out of context it is. These buildings, marching across downtown Albany like something out of *The War of The Worlds*, are in the city but not of it. Weighing in at $2 billion worth of marble and ego, they invite comparison with the State Capitol and with City Hall. Henry Hobson Richardson, too, built on a monumental scale, but with a human sense of detail. The Mall buildings seem meant for men 50 feet tall, with no eye for anything but the clean stark line.

The argument has been made that the South Mall sparked the revival of downtown Albany, that adjacent,

SAMUEL WILSON
Died July 31, 1854
Aged 88 Years

rapidly after the introduction of sewing machines in the 1850s. The industry was long-lived; as recently as 1940, a single Troy shirtmaker employed 3,700 workers. The local steel business wasn't as fortunate: in 1863 a Troy concern became the first American company licensed to make and sell Bessemer-process steel, but just 10 years later Andrew Carnegie set up shop in Pittsburgh and stole Troy's ground-floor position in the material that would build the 20th century.

No longer America's shirt and collar capital, and with its other traditional industries having long since experienced the decline characteristic of the smokestack towns of the Northeast in the postwar era, Troy's job in recent years has been to avoid slipping into a "rustbelt" stereotype—in reality no less that in popular perception. One important asset in the

"Uncle Sam" Wilson was among those who moved the center of American prosperity westward from the old colonial coast.

CHRIS MAYNARD PHOTOS BOTH PAGES

Right: *A granddaughter's monument to a nation's "uncle."*
Facing page: *Sculpture in downtown Troy honors the mythological Uncle Sam.*

struggle has been Rensselaer Polytechnic Institute (RPI). Founded in 1824 by the "last patroon," Stephen van Rensselaer, RPI has grown to become one of the nation's most highly regarded institutions of scientific and technological training. Rensselaer's campus dominates central Troy from the heights of Mt. Ida overlooking the Hudson River, but its commitment to carrying its hometown across the difficult bridge from the shirt-and-steel industrial past to the postindustrial future is best exemplified by its leadership role in creating the new Rensselaer Technical Park, a center for high-tech enterprises on the outskirts of the city.

Among Troy's other assets are extensive blocks of Civil-War–era brick rowhouses, prime for rehabilitation by state government workers and other professionals looking for alternatives to the pricier residential neighborhoods of Albany, and a compact downtown in which ancient taverns with signs that still say "Ladies' Entrance" are now crowded by chic little restaurants and raw-seafood bars.

On one of those downtown streets near the Troy waterfront stands a modern statue representing Troy's most famous citizen: Samuel Wilson, the real-life "Uncle Sam." The story goes that when Wilson, a Troy meatpacker, was given a contract to supply American troops with provisions during the War of 1812, the "U.S." (for "United States") stamped on his barrels of government-consigned salt beef was said by local soldiers to stand for "Uncle Sam." While no evidence exists to suggest that Wilson resembled the gangly, white-goateed character that came to personify the United States, the Troy statue shows him looking very much like the popular icon. The real source of Uncle Sam's appearance was early 19th century cartoonists' common caricature of New England rustics, and the old man's stars and stripes outfit was suggested by a costume worn by a local zany in a long-ago Fourth of July parade in Amesbury, Massachusetts. Samuel Wilson, himself, in fact, was a native of Arlington, a town just west of Boston. But there is no need for New England to try to steal Uncle Sam back from Troy. After all, the meatpacker Samuel Wilson did head west to the Hudson Valley to seek his fortune, as part of the great wave of entrepreneurs, farmers and laborers who succeeded in moving the geographic center of American prosperity from the old colonial coast to New York State.

THE EAST SHORE SOUTH OF ALBANY

4

The Franklin Delano Roosevelt home at Hyde Park.

CHRIS MAYNARD

Five New York counties lie to the east of the Hudson River, extending from a latitude roughly even with Vermont's southern border to the northern reaches of New York City's suburbs. Here the grandest of the valley's mansions still sentinel the shore, while the rolling country that begins at their front doors rises gently toward the worn green summits of the Berkshire and Taconic hills. This narrow stretch of land, seldom measuring more than 20 miles from the river to the borders of Connecticut and Massachusetts, is more than just the geographical meeting place of New York and New England; it represents a melding of the characters of the two regions as well. Especially in the northern part of the counties east of the Hudson, among the farms and hill towns at Troy's back door, you get the distinct feeling that the boundary line between New York and Vermont represents one of the world's more arbitrary political divisions. (New Yorkers felt so, too, more than 200 years ago, which is why Ethan Allen and his Green Mountain Boys dedicated themselves to throwing out "Yorker" surveyors.) This is the country painted by Anna Mary Robertson Moses, known to the world as Grandma.

Anna Robertson was born on a farm in Washington County, New York in 1860. She married Thomas Moses when she was only 17 and moved to Virginia, where her 10 children were born. In 1905, the family returned to New York State, settling on a farm near Hoosick Falls. Here Grandma Moses spent the rest of her life.

In 1938, when she was 78, Grandma Moses began to paint. She was entirely self-taught, and at that her education ran only to the practical aspects of her medium and not at all to the history of the western world's art—not even to the American folk style of which she is now regarded as the last ingenuous master. She painted the farm and small-town life that she knew so well from her years in the upper Hudson Valley, and although the subject of her pictures has changed in its particulars, her hills and villages are still recognizable to anyone who drives the back roads of the border country. Grandma Moses first exhibited her works in a drugstore in Hoosick Falls, and she was almost immediately discovered by the American art establishment. She painted prolifically throughout the remaining two decades of her life, and died in 1961 at the age of 101.

The idealized, pre-industrial life of husbandry and simple domestic arts that exists at the core of Grandma Moses' paintings were the concepts that fired the practitioners of a famous socio-religious movement that once had its headquarters in the upper Hudson Valley. The United Society of Believers in Christ's Second Appearing was a quietist sect founded in England by a woman named Mother Ann Lee and introduced to New York State in the 1780s. Nicknamed "Shakers" after their physical approach to prayer, the American members of the sect established their motherhouse at Mt. Lebanon. Here, as at their other communal centers in New England, the Shakers lived their life of work and prayer, of sublimation of worldly desires and of sharing all things except the pleasures of the flesh. The Shakers were celibate. Their numbers never exceeded 6,000, even during their peak years in the mid-1800s, and of course such expansion as the

Above and right: The joy of simplicity at the Shaker Museum, Chatham.

sect once enjoyed was the result of adult conversion rather than of Shakers-to-be being born to believers. Today there are perhaps a half-dozen, and the Mt. Lebanon motherhouse has long since vanished.

But the Shakers were concerned just enough with material things to have left a remarkable legacy of crafts-manship. They made household items such as boxes, furniture and simple tools with such utilitarian grace that today the term "Shaker" is more apt to conjure a style of design than a religion or philosophy of life. And in this regard, the upper Hudson Valley is still a seat of Shakerism: at Old Chatham, in the Taconic foothills halfway between the river and Pittsfield, Massachusetts, a Shaker Museum has preserved more than 35,000 of the sect's artifacts and re-created the gardens and workshops that were the hubs of Shaker life a century and a half ago. The overall effect is enough to make Grandma Moses' work seem downright lively and sophisticated; to some of us, an excess of simplicity is as bad as an excess of anything

else (or worse, depending). But it is no surprise that the green hills of the upper valley nurtured both the communal co-religionists and, a hundred years later, the old widow with her paintbrushes. A certain pastoral vision of America, then and now, seldom finds a landscape as congenial as this one.

Three roads, and the palace of an American artist

Three principal north-south routes run through the sliver of New York that lies between the Hudson and New England. State Route 22 meanders down along the western shore of Lake Champlain and drifts into the Taconic Mountains south of Hoosick Falls; then for over a hundred miles it skirts the borders of Massachusetts and Connecticut, touching on one Norman Rockwell town after another before finally losing itself among the bedroom suburbs and corporate headquarters of Westchester County. Down the center of the strip runs a road that reveals the best of the region's rolling scenery without passing through the towns. This is the Taconic State Parkway, which begins in Chatham at the New York Thruway–Massachusetts Turnpike connector (roughly opposite Pittsfield, Massachusetts) and finishes just north of New York City. The Taconic is a throwback to the earliest days of four-lane highway construction in America. It is narrow by modern standards; it has very little in the way of shoulders; and the way it snakes through the countryside reminds you more of a two-lane blacktop than of anything labeled a "parkway." Most disconcerting of all, to the uninitiated driver, is the fact that this is not really a "limited access" road at all—all manner of secondary routes merge with and even cross the Taconic. Fortunately, it is not very heavily traveled. All this said, the Taconic cannot be more highly recommended. It follows a route that beautifully integrates the valley itself with the uplands to the east, and at several points along its northern section the road rises to reveal magnificent vistas of the Catskills looming above the glinting Hudson. I drove the upper Taconic once as a terrific thunderstorm gathered, and concluded that Washington Irving's reference to the old Dutch legend of Henry Hudson and his men playing ninepins among the clouds might not be so implausible. And I also decided that this might be the most beautiful river valley in the world.

Farthest west among the three main pathways of the east valley is U.S. Route 9 and its alphabet-soup relations— 9J, 9G, 9D and 9A, unless we've missed a few. Route 9G runs right along the Hudson, and is the most unmistakeably "New York" of the three north-south routes. Along with its alternatives, it winds along the riverbank at or near water level, through old Dutch towns dating to the days of the patroons and through small brick cities gambling on economic revival. It passes directly by those of the old Hudson Valley money as well as the mansions of the newer, turn-of-the-century money that played at being old. And just 35 miles south of Troy, outside the town of Hudson, it passes by a steep drive leading up to the most architecturally exotic, and quite possibly the loveliest, of all the great houses on the Hudson: Frederic Edwin Church's Olana.

"About an hour this side of Albany is the center of the world," Frederic Church once wrote. "I own it." As the

On the porch at Frederic Church's home, Olana.

Frederic Church was never the type of artist to starve in a garret.

Right: Frederic Church's view of the Hudson from Olana.
Facing page: Inside and out, Olana is a Persian fantasy.

foremost landscape painter of his day, Church was no mean judge of beautiful scenery—but it was more than just the Hudson River and Catskill vistas from his hilltop property that occasioned his proud declaration. The center of Church's world was Olana, the 37-room Persian mansion that he designed and decorated himself.

Frederic Church was never the type of artist to starve in a garret. The son of a well-to-do businessman, he studied under the Hudson River School master Thomas Cole and gained wealth and fame early in his career through the exhibition and sale of monumental landscapes such as *The Heart of the Andes* and *Niagara*. By the early 1860s, he and his wife Isabel had moved to a farm just south of Hudson, where the artist could draw inspiration from the property's "most beautiful and wonderful" views of the valley.

But Church had even grander visions in mind, along with a house far more extravagant than the cottage Richard Morris Hunt had designed for the farm. In 1867, he added an adjacent hilltop to his acreage and commissioned Hunt to crown it with a French chateau. Later that same year, though, Church took his family on a two-year tour of Europe and the Near East—and when he returned, nothing so tame as the Hunt chateau would suit his fancy. He had fallen under the spell of the Levant, of the rich colors, floral intricacies and lush geometry of the Islamic

decorative arts. Church would have an Orientalist's dream of a Persian palace. He replaced Hunt with the architect Calvert Vaux, but the man who really designed and finished Olana was the artist himself.

Church and his family moved into Olana in 1872, but the house and its grounds remained a work-in-progress virtually until his death in 1900. Within the hilltop house, with its walls of dressed stone and polychrome brick and its stout mansarded minaret (Church drew all the colored-slate patterns himself), this supreme aesthete-collector piled up an amazing collection of Persian carpets, Japanese bronzes, Tiffany glass, Chinese tables, Indian woodcarvings and intricate stencilwork that adorned interior walls with mosaic-like designs and Arabic script. Sunlight fell upon these carefully cluttered spaces through amber window glass, and often was subtly reflected by deftly placed mirrors.

The grounds of Olana were, to Church, no less a canvas than the house and its contents. He cut trees to open vistas and planted others to frame them, all the while positioning the property's roads and paths to take maximum advantage of the manicured foreground and the sublime, untamed views of the river and the Catskill Mountains. For a Hudson River School painter to have lived in this relation to the source of so much of his inspiration is akin to Charles Russell or Frederick Remington having owned a great piece of Montana, or to Utrillo being the mayor of Montparnasse.

Incredibly, Olana was nearly demolished. Church's daughter-in-law lived in the house until her death in 1964, at

CHRIS MAYNARD PHOTOS BOTH PAGES

Above and facing page:
Clermont, rebuilt after the British burned it in 1777, housed members of the Livingston family for almost two centuries afterwards.

Church's 300-plus acres seem like a suburban subdivision. Virtually the entire southern third of Columbia County—160,000 acres—was chartered in 1686 as the Manor of Livingston, personal fiefdom of the clever Scot Robert Livingston who married so well into the van Rensselaer family. Upon the first Lord of the Manor's death in 1728, the 13,000-acre tract known as the "Lower Manor" (near present-day Germantown) was inherited by his third son, also named Robert. With a medieval flair that has an odd ring to it in the New World, Livingston II called himself Robert of Clermont, after the common name for the Lower Manor. Clermont was also the name of his house, which he built in 1730 on high ground looking west across the river.

Two Roberts later, Robert R. Livingston—Robert of Clermont's grandson—rebuilt the family home after it was burned by British troops during the Hudson Valley campaign of 1777. This was the house as Robert Fulton knew it when he courted Livingston's daughter, and its name—Clermont—was the one which logically appealed to him for the steamboat that he launched upon the Hudson with Livingston's backing in 1807.

Clermont still stands; in fact, it was the home of a branch of the Livingston family until as recently as 1962. In that year the house and its antique furnishings, along with a last vestige of the Lower Manor—a not inconsiderable 500 acres of parklike river frontage—were acquired by the state. Today the property forms the northernmost jewel in a string of now-publicly–owned estates built by the barons of the Hudson (we're not counting Olana; Church was an artist first and a baron second) and perhaps is the most illustrative of the feudal style of the east shore landholders. Later magnates such as Ogden Mills and Jay Gould may have set themselves up in quasi-royal circumstances, but only at Clermont did you get the real prerevolutionary impression of an aristocracy based upon landholding rather than success in industry or commerce. The Livingston who worked with Fulton was something of a transitional character in this regard: lord of so much land along the Hudson, he sought immense profits by helping to develop and monopolize a new means of travel upon it. We saw earlier what Cornelius Vanderbilt thought of that idea—and his descendants built a riverside mansion even bigger than Clermont.

The road south from Livingston's old estate to the Vanderbilt Mansion leads through the old town of Rhinebeck, which bears a German rather than a Dutch name because it was the settling place of many of the Rhineland Palatine families

which time the great white elephant and its contents were put up for sale. There was little hope that a new buyer would preserve the aging, money-absorbing structure, until an organization called Olana Preservation was formed and collected sufficient funds to exercise an option to purchase. The private group held the house and grounds for acquisition by the state of New York, which assumed membership in 1966 at the strong urging of Gov. Nelson Rockefeller. Now that Olana has been beautifully restored and opened to visitors, we can be thankful that the ego responsible for Albany's Empire State Plaza was at least appreciative of another larger-than-life character's magnificent obsession.

Stops along the Valley: Mansions, an ancient inn, and a duel above the western front

The river's east shore along Route 9G south of Hudson, along with much of the hinterlands reaching back into the Taconic Hills, were once part of an estate that made Frederic who emigrated to the Hudson Valley early in the 18th century. Thirty-five of those families settled in Rhinebeck in 1715, just 15 years after William Traphagen built a two-room stone tavern in what was to become the center of the village, where an old Indian trail to the river crossed the King's Highway. That humble inn was the predecessor of a two-story fieldstone hostelry built by Traphagen's son, Arent, in 1766. The second building survives, with several later additions, as the Beekman Arms, now the oldest lodging-place in the United States.

The Beekman Arms (it was named for the Beekman family, original owners of the land it stands on) is not a country inn in the modern sense of a big single-family home transformed via chintz and antiques into a weekend retreat. It is instead a rare bit of living history, a colonial tavern with comfortable rooms for travelers. The walls are two feet thick, and the wide-plank floors creak agreeably; a fire crackles on the great hearth in the entry hall as it did for Alexander Hamilton and the Marquis de Lafayette. You cannot lift the worn iron latch in the immense front door without feeling the heft of time and the solace of continuity with the past; it is no wonder that Franklin Roosevelt came to this ancient social center of his shire for one last rally on each of the election nights that delivered him the governorship of New York and the presidency of the United States.

History of a very different sort has been transplanted and brought to life in another corner of Rhinebeck. The Old Rhinebeck Aerodrome may be on the east bank of the Hudson, but in spirit it is located on the Western Front in the days of Rickenbacker and von Richtofen. The Aerodrome is the creation of one man, Cole Palen, who has managed to fulfill the barnstorming ambitions of his youth while at the same time amassing a collection of more than 60 real and reproduction aircraft covering the three decades of flying's infancy and youth. Best of all, both the planes and their irrepressible flying owner are on public display from spring to fall of each year.

Not content merely to show off museum pieces such as a Sopwith Camel complete with bomb releases, or a 1918 Curtiss Jenny, Palen set up his operation as a working aerodrome, complete with hangars that could have been props in *Those Magnificent Men and Their Flying Machines* and a grassy airstrip lined with false-front buildings suggestive of a town somewhere near the Front. Despite the fact that, as one of his assistants told me, "each hour of flight means an

CHRIS MAYNARD PHOTOS BOTH PAGES

Above: Looking much like 18th century England, the Mills Mansion at Staatsburg is now a state historic site.
Right: At the Old Rhinebeck Aerodrome.
Facing page: View of the Hudson from the grounds of the Frederick Vanderbilt estate, which is open to the public.

average of thirteen and a half hours of maintenance and repair," Palen and his pilots take off each week in a slapstick reworking of the evil-Prussian-meets-stalwart-Allied-flyer legend, with the boss himself playing the role of the "Black Baron." For those who cannot get enough of the barnstorming spirit while remaining earthbound, a pair of reliable 1929 New Standards D-25s are kept on hand to take visitors aloft. If there is a better way to see the Hudson Valley countryside than by driving the Taconic Parkway with the top down, this is it. On a New Standard D-25, the top is always down.

The section of Route 9 that stretches along the river from Rhinebeck to Poughkeepsie is mansion country, with sights more suggestive of an era irrevocably gone by than any Fokker or Sopwith. This is where an ersatz patroonship could be bought with a killing on the market or with one's profits from the Machiavellian railroad gambits of the Gilded Age. Here, in Staatsburg, the financier Ogden Mills hired the architectural firm of McKim, Mead, and White, masters of the classical revival, to update and enlarge a Greek Revival house that had been in his wife's family for several generations. (Mrs. Mills was a Livingston, and as such was no stranger to lordly riverfront residences.) When Messrs. White and company were finished in 1896, they left behind a structure that looked less like a Hudson Valley country seat than an 18th-century great house in the English countryside. The Mills Mansion, as it has been known officially since becoming a state historic site following the death of U.S. Treasury Secretary Ogden L. Mills, son of the builder, is a columned and pilastered extravaganza that may well have reminded the younger Mills of his office building in Washington—the one on the back of the $10 bill. The formality of the interior of the Mills Mansion is a perfect match for the classical facade; the Mills' taste leaned toward Louis XV and XVI, Flemish tapestries and gilt plaster moldings: it is a long way from Hoosick Falls (as in Grandma Moses) to Staatsburg.

Just south of Staatsburg, in Hyde Park, McKim, Mead, and White executed an even grander commission for Frederick W Vanderbilt, grandson of the Commodore. The Vanderbilt Mansion, now a national historic site, is a 50-room Italian Renaissance villa completed in 1899 at a cost of $2.25 million, including furnishings and improvement of the grounds. The great stone house, with its columned porticoes and elaborately carved and bemuraled interiors (many of the details were shipped over from France, where they had graced a chateau once owned by Napoleon I) was only a part-time residence of Mr. and Mrs.

Vanderbilt; nevertheless, it represents as well as any other architectural artifact of the Hudson Valley the ducal style that descended on the region in the high-water days of untaxed American capitalism. Here, on just more than 200 riverfront acres, the Vanderbilts maintained not only their mansion but also a working farm that amounted to a business of considerable size. What other non-industrial enterprise in these parts has employed 60 people? And that was *after* construction was finished. It took 13 men just to care for the estate's lawns and gardens, and a crew of 17 to staff the four floors of the mansion. Frederick Vanderbilt sat on the boards of 22 railroads, but his real life's work would seem to have been the maintenance of his households.

The feudal touch even extended to a certain *noblesse oblige* in the relationship of the Vanderbilts to the Hyde Park community. Mrs. Vanderbilt sent coal and fuel to poor families and paid for the schooling of local girls who might show promise. She underwrote the costs of the local young men's club and gave ice cream parties for village children. At Christmas, she handed out toys to needy youngsters. Mr. Vanderbilt sponsored a town lecture series and helped finance the local home defense company during World War I. When the town needed a new stone bridge over Crum Elbow Creek, he contributed $18,000 for its construction.

The Valley's greatest shrine

This apogee of America's self-made aristocracy, so conspicuous in charity (at least in the Vanderbilts' case) and in consumption, lasted barely more than a generation. By the time Frederick Vanderbilt died in 1938, having achieved an age of 82 years and a net worth of $78 million, the private palaces of the Hudson Valley were well past their golden age. Having died childless, Vanderbilt left his estate to a niece, but she kept it only for two years before donating it to the federal government and consigning it to the curious stares of five decades of tourists.

In that same year of 1940, the government also took possession of a 16-acre parcel of another estate, just south of the Vanderbilt property, on which a private foundation had built a special museum and library—one devoted to the sitting president of the United States whose home stood on the adjacent grounds. Five years later, when Franklin Delano Roosevelt died early in his fourth term of office, the entire Roosevelt estate became property of the American people.

"Springwood" **(above)**, *FDR's birthplace, and inside the Vanderbilt mansion* **(right)**— *never the twain shall meet.*

Franklin Roosevelt's Hudson Valley connections were quite different from those of Frederick Vanderbilt. Both men, of course, were New York Dutch with 17th-century New Netherlands antecedents; but while Vanderbilt—grandson of Staten Island's Commodore—had bought his Hyde Park property in order to build his mansion there, FDR was the product of four generations of Roosevelts and Delanos who had lived on or near the river. His mother had grown up on an estate near Newburgh, and his father, James Roosevelt, inherited a family home at Hyde Park in 1848. After that house burned in 1866, the elder Roosevelt purchased Springwood, the property on which the present mansion—much altered in the course of a 1915 enlargement and remodeling—already stood. Franklin D. Roosevelt was born in an upstairs bedroom of this house on January 30, 1882.

An anecdote illustrates the difference between the Roosevelts and the Vanderbilts in the Hudson Valley scheme of things far better than a simple comparison of length of tenure on their two pieces of real estate. According to the story, James and Sara Roosevelt were invited to a dinner at the Vanderbilt Mansion just after it was completed in 1899. Mrs. Roosevelt wanted to go; the building and landscaping that had been going on for two years on the Vanderbilt estate were the talk of Dutchess County. But Franklin Roosevelt's father said no, he did not care to attend the dinner. His reason? If he and his wife were to accept the invitation, they would have to reciprocate by welcoming "these people" into their own home.

Although James Roosevelt himself sat on the corporate boards of railroads and was no stranger to the heady environment of post–Civil War American business, he really belonged to a different era as well as a different social order than the Vanderbilt scions. Born in 1828 and already in his 50s when Franklin was born (his first marriage, which had also produced a son, had ended with his wife's death in 1876), he came out of a landed, pre-industrial tradition of squires on horseback rather than boardroom operators. He was one of the last of the old well-to-do country Dutchmen, secure in his family beyond the need for ostentation.

The real contrast was with Franklin. The boy James Roosevelt raised in his happy old age was really at least two generations removed from him, rather than one; while the father was in many ways a man of the early 19th century, the son turned out to be one of the inventors of the 20th.

Not that Franklin Roosevelt did not nearly become a squire at Hyde Park himself. Although he began a political career (much to his mother's dismay) with election to the New York State Senate in 1910 and quickly rose to become assistant secretary of the Navy and Democratic candidate for vice president in the election of 1920, his devastating bout with polio in the following year left him with the prospect of spending the rest of his days looking after his estate from a wheelchair. His mother, strong as ever to the point of being domineering, favored exactly such a future for her son. But FDR could not face retirement at 40, and paralyzed though he was he worked with his wife Eleanor and his friend and advisor Louis Howe to chart the course that took him to the New York governorship in 1928 and the presidency in 1932.

Although he opted against being its prisoner, Hyde Park always remained FDR's solace. "All that is within me cries out to go back to my home on the Hudson River," the president wrote during the war years, and although he was never to enjoy the retirement he longed for he did return often, accompanied by the weight of the world, and by more than a few of its leaders. It was during these years that he decided to bequeath his estate to the government, with an option of life tenure for his wife and children. When they waived that right, Hyde Park the home became Hyde Park the shrine. FDR, and later Eleanor Roosevelt, were buried in the Rose Garden on the grounds.

The Roosevelt Museum makes for a tour of hours, even a day. Its treasures range from young Franklin's wicker pony saddle and the family iceboat to the president's oval desk and specimens of correspondence relative to the New Deal, the Second World War and the dawn of the Atomic Age. Eleanor Roosevelt's career is also amply documented, both at the museum and at her private retreat, Val-Kill, elsewhere on the estate. By contrast the house itself seems almost

Picnicking in Poughkeepsie.

Although he opted against being its prisoner, Hyde Park always remained FDR's solace.

anticlimactic. Except for a couple of grand, antique-filled downstairs rooms, Springwood is much like the typical middle-class residences of its day, only larger—until you begin to sense the spirit that fills the upstairs rooms and to imagine what went over the wire from that bedside telephone. One small bedroom suggests a boy just gone to Harvard, while across the hallway Winston Churchill was a guest nearly half a century later. Here in the pleasant domestic milieu of the Hudson Valley gentry old James Roosevelt steered his fortune and his family as effortlessly as he steered his yacht; but here, as much as in the White House or the map rooms beneath London, the survival of civilization was determined.

The lower Valley: Poughkeepsie and points south

If James Roosevelt thought that the Vanderbilts were questionable neighbors, he was fortunate not to have lived into the age of fast food and strip malls. Just outside the gates of Springwood the northern reaches of Poughkeepsie begin, appropriately (ironically?) enough with the Roosevelt cinema and the Roosevelt motel. Just down the road is a somewhat more august institution, the Culinary Institute of America. The Institute is one of the nation's premier schools for the training of chefs and regularly sends graduates on to careers in the finest hotels and restaurants. Part of the curriculum involves working in the on-campus restaurant, which is open to the public five days a week. The prices are reasonable, the menu *au courant,* and the quality of the food and service quite professional.

Right: A work session at Culinary Institute of America in Poughkeepsie.
Far right: Vassar College, Poughkeepsie.

The Poughkeepsie campus, purchased by the Culinary Institute when it moved here from Connecticut in the early 1970s, was for many years a Jesuit seminary, one of several in the Hudson Valley. In a small Jesuit cemetery adjacent to the property is the grave of the once-controversial French paleontologist-theologian Father Pierre Teilhard de Chardin. Teilhard is probably the most influential Catholic thinker to be buried behind a cooking school: our world, as he made clear in his writings, continues to evolve.

Poughkeepsie is also the home of Vassar College, once the *ne plus ultra* of higher education for young ladies and the leading light of the female Ivy League known as the "Seven Sisters." Now in its second decade of admitting men and approaching numerical parity between the sexes, Vassar has set itself the mission of being a first-rate liberal arts college, period, rather than the premier liberal arts college for women. Inasmuch as its physical surroundings help set the tone for academic accomplishment, the resources remain the same: a gorgeous 1,000-acre campus encompassing 200 species of trees, two lakes, an ecological preserve and an outdoor amphitheater. If you cannot live on a Hudson River estate, with the right transcript and board scores you can at least rent one for four years.

And what of Poughkeepsie itself? None but the most shameless booster would suggest that it has not seen better days, like most of the mid-size communities of the valley; nevertheless, the strong hand of International Business Machines is guiding at least one segment of the population and economy into more prosperous times. In the middle of an undeniably faded downtown stands a big new hotel-convention center complex, and rightly or wrongly those things are always the opening volley in any campaign to turn a town around. During a stay at the hotel a few months after it opened, however, I found a whimsical bit of self-deprecation right in the gift shop—just the place where you would expect to see coffee mugs saying the place was the Paris of the Hudson. This souvenir was a T-shirt bearing the legend: "Poughkeepsie: Only the Strong Survive." Did they mean that only the strong survive in Poughkeepsie , or that Poughkeepsie itself would survive because it was strong? As a clue, I would hate to take the graffiti evidence of the existence of a social organization called the "Cro-Mags," proclaimed on one of the stone foundations of Poughkeepsie's immense, abandoned railroad bridge. It is a fine hotel, in any event.

For most of the nine miles from Poughkeepsie to the old mill town of Wappingers Falls, Route 9 is a drab commercial strip. But south of Wappingers Falls travelers who are not in a hurry have the option of following 9D along the river through Beacon, clustered beneath abrupt, 1,600-foot Mt. Beacon. People hereabouts are aware that in truly mountainous parts of the country nothing a mere 1,600 feet high would rate even as a hill, but Mt. Beacon is the northern sentinel, on the east bank, of a stretch of scenery far more dramatic than mere altitude might suggest. This is the Hudson Highlands, a precipitous sequence of domes and cliffs and tors, as the Dutch called them, that frames both sides of the Hudson Gorge above Haverstraw Bay and the Tappan Zee and gives it its Rhinelike grandeur.

The Highlands are best appreciated from the middle of the river itself, but if a trip on an excursion vessel or private boat is not feasible, a vantage point at water level on either side is nearly as good. One such choice might be Garrison's Landing, where a side road off 9D dead-ends at a little marina, a train station converted to a venue for the local theater company and a cluster of nondescript houses with an art gallery in their midst. The hamlet looks like some quirky construction in a model train layout and the Hudson is so close you could fall in. Across the water are the stone bastions of the United States Military Academy at West Point, giving

In the middle of Poughkeepsie, a big new hotel-convention center is the beginning volley in a campaign to turn the town around.

Top: *The Rhinebeck Inn, downtown Rhinebeck, is the oldest inn in the nation.*
Left: *The Masonic Lodge of Rhinebeck hosts a lobster dinner.*

63

Above: The waterfront at Garrison's Landing, an excellent place from which to view the Hudson Highlands.
Right: The First Reformed Dutch Church at Fishkill was built in 1731.

way on the north to the brooding mass of Storm King. To the south, the Hudson Gorge—the fjord—narrows as it approaches the gap spanned by the Bear Mountain Bridge. The bridge, too, is a good place to get a view of the Highlands. Along with auto traffic, it carries the Appalachian Trail across the river from Palisades Interstate Park to the bluff rock face of 900-foot Anthony's Nose, beyond which the trail meanders eastward toward the Hudson Highlands Park and the Connecticut border. No one seems certain how the "Nose" got its name—some explanations lean towards St. Anthony, for some obscure reason, while others mention Peter Stuyvesant's trumpeter, Anthony Corlear—but the steep formation that anchors the end of the Bear Mountain Bridge is generally agreed upon as the southern portal of the Hudson Highlands proper.

One inescapable aspect of the topography of the east shore at water level, throughout the Highlands as well as to the north and south, is the ubiquitous trackage of the New York Central, now a part of the Conrail system. Poke down any back road to the river's edge, to Garrison or any of dozens of other small towns, and the high iron is the last thing you will see before the water. It presses on past mansion and shack alike, sometimes as many as four tracks abreast: the Commodore's right-of-way has dominated the waterfront between Manhattan and Albany for well over a century. But while it does get in the way of public access and parkland (except at places like Croton Point Park, which projects past the tracks into the river), the railroad's presence has actually been called a blessing as well as a curse by some Hudson River environmentalists. The reason? As long as the tracks dominate the shore, there is less likelihood that it will be developed. It is an ill wind that blows no one good.

Harmon, a small community on Haverstraw Bay south of Peekskill and just north of Croton Point, was an important division point on the New York Central railroad. It was here that electric engines on northbound trains were exchanged for steam, and later diesel, locomotives; the operation of smoky steam engines had been prohibited on Manhattan Island in the first decade of this century. The process, of course, would be reversed on southbound trains, which made Harmon the site of one of the great stables of steam. It was here that the Chicago-bound *Twentieth Century Limited* would be coupled to motive power commensurate with its grandeur—the mighty, eight-drivered titans named "Hudsons" after the water level route they traveled. In those days, small boys up and down the valley would listen each night for the blast of a steam whistle, knowing that the

Century would be right on time at each point along the river leg of its 900-mile, 16-hour race to Chicago.

The Hudson Valley meets the metropolis: Westchester

Westchester, the county in which Harmon is located, is also in a sense the creation of the railroads—not as a way station, but as a destination for commuter trains. As such it has fallen into the metropolitan vernacular along with Long Island as a synonym for split-level suburbia, with all its sociological baggage. It is even a literary landscape, peopled by the commuting heroes of one-time Ossining resident John Cheever's novels and short stories. But the Cheever characters are not from Westchester; they merely live there because it is a convenient bedroom adjacent to their jobs in the city. Thus fiction, along with generally accepted stereotype, tends to obscure the fact that anyone was ever from Westchester, or that it indeed has a history and character of its own. Mention White Plains, and no one thinks of the Continental Army's desperate battle to avoid entrapment. Mention New Rochelle, and who would immediately think of it as the home of the revolutionary pamphleteer Thomas Paine? Anyone who did might flash a quick mental image of Paine riding the 5:47 out of Grand Central, maybe handing out copies of *Common Sense* to his fellow commuters. Scarsdale is a diet, not a town, and Armonk could almost go down on the map as simply IBM—it is the computer leviathan's world headquarters.

Of course there was a Westchester before there were commuter trains and exurban corporate offices. It was a county of cleared, rolling farmland back when the outer suburbs of the metropolis were still somewhere on Manhattan Island. It was the sort of country place to which a man like John Jay might retire. Jay, a governor of New York, co-author of *The Federalist Papers* and first chief justice of the U.S. Supreme Court, lived the last 28 years of his life on his 900-acre Katonah farm. When the last of his descendants to live on the property died in 1953, the house and remaining grounds became a state historic site.

The countryside between Katonah and the Hudson River was still quite rural in 1892 when work began on what was billed as the "eighth wonder of the world"—the New Croton Dam on the northern outskirts of Ossining. The 2,600-foot dam rises to a height of 290 feet and holds back the waters of the Croton River in a 32-billion-gallon reservoir

that floods a serpentine valley reaching back a dozen miles to Katonah. Katonah, in fact, had to be moved to accommodate the man-made lake. Most of the work on the New Croton Dam was done by immigrants from Sicily and southern Italy, whose descendants still comprise a considerable portion of the population of Westchester. And the reservoir is still the principal link in New York City's water supply, its water entering the smaller receiving reservoir in Central Park, Manhattan, by way of a cavernous underground conduit—the Hudson's invisible alter-ego south of Ossining.

Although another Ossining institution, Sing Sing state prison (the original destination implied in the phrase, "up the river"), is perhaps the best-known man-made landmark along this stretch of the Hudson, the real character and historical depth of the lower valley is best revealed in a pair of public places south of the Tappan Zee Bridge. The first is Sunnyside, beloved home of America's first well known author and ardent chronicler of the valley's earliest white settlers, Washington Irving. Sunnyside is located in Tarrytown, a

At Cold Spring, which affords views of the brooding Storm King.

Visitors to Sunnyside today may feel as if Washington Irving had not left too long ago.

Sunnyside, Washington Irving's home.

contrivance, there can be no doubt about his house; it is. The structure that became Sunnyside was built by a Dutch farmer around 1690 and was little more than a ruin when Irving acquired it. The house he made of it he later described as "a little old-fashioned stone mansion, all made up of gable ends, and as full of angles and corners as an old cocked hat." It was an antiquarian's house, sure enough, a step-gabled throwback to the era its owner chronicled in *Diedrich Knickerbocker's History of New York.* Irving retired here, if the busy life he lived can be called retirement, from 1836 to 1842 and again from 1846 until his death in 1859. To visit Sunnyside today is to get the impression that he has not left all that long ago—everything, from the personally designed orchards and gardens to the study with the writing desk at which *Astoria* and *The Life of George Washington* were set down, suggests the palpable presence of Washington Irving. It was enough of a presence, while he was here, to leave no doubt about how the next town down the river got its name: just south of Tarrytown, along the Tappan Zee, is Irvington.

The other Westchester treasure intimately linked with the lower valley and its history is the Hudson River Museum in Yonkers. The museum, which since 1923 has been housed in the 1876 Eastlake-style Trevor Mansion overlooking the river, has assigned itself an eclectic mission ranging from planetarium shows to exhibits of contemporary local artists. But at its core it is a celebration of the natural and social history, art and architecture, and general flavor of life as it has been lived along this part of the Hudson. It includes paintings by Jasper Cropsey and Albert Bierstadt; an inventory of local architecture; and a collection of Westchester minerals. The effect is to add temporal depth to a region whose history, as is common with suburban places, is all too often thought of in terms of yesterday or the day before. The shadows of the next town down the river from Yonkers tend to obscure Long Island, northern New Jersey and anything else that gets near them. It's been that way since that town was called New Amsterdam.

village whose name Irving himself offered to interpret. According to the author, the "tarry" in Tarrytown referred to the Dutch farmers' habit of loafing at the local tavern after bringing produce to the market; the town, he said, was named by their disapproving wives. A less colorful explanation has it that "tarry" comes from the Dutch word *tarwe* for wheat, which was formerly grown in the area.

While some may question whether Washington Irving's etymology for the name of his adopted town is a whimsical

Above: *The appropriately stark lines of a Sing Sing guards' tower near Ossining.*
Left: *The town of Ossining presents a pleasant 19th-century aspect.*
Far left: *Croton Reservoir near Ossining is a main source of water for New York City.*

THE WEST SHORE AND THE EASTERN CATSKILLS

The broad and placid Hudson near Newburgh Bridge.

CHRIS MAYNARD

If you want to see the west shore of the Hudson, stay off the New York State Thruway. The Thruway, officially known as the Thomas E. Dewey Thruway after the punctilious governor and twice-failed presidential candidate, does a wonderful job of shrinking the distance between the Jersey line and Albany—but it does so by slighting both the river and the Catskills. Far better, if you are out for scenery, history and the true colors of the valley, to follow a slow road like 9W, with appropriate forays west into the mountains.

Actually, the best way to begin exploring the western side of the valley is to start out on foot, in New Jersey, at a spot that lies nearly in the shadows of the George Washington Bridge. This is where the state-protected section of the Palisades begins, along with the trails that offer routes either atop the cliffs or at water level.

"Protected" is a key word here. While the Palisades might seem inviolable, save perhaps for the kind of overdevelopment that characterizes their southern extreme at Fort Lee, they were very nearly reduced to rubble and carted away a hundred years ago.

The responsible parties were quarry operators, who were busily blasting away at the cliffs in order to obtain crushed stone for asphalt paving and other projects under way in the fast-growing metropolitan area. Having seen the southernmost reaches of the Palisades virtually demolished, concerned citizens on both sides of the Hudson began looking for a way to save the remainder. The solution came through the formation of a joint commission on the part of the states of New Jersey and New York, and the appropriation by both legislatures of $15,000 in seed money to begin acquisition of the cliffs and their river frontage. The remaining funds were to come from private contributions. The largest donation, $122,500, was submitted by J.P. Morgan. By the end of 1900, the last of the quarrying businesses had been purchased and the destruction of the Palisades had been ended. Ten years of smaller acquisitions followed—including the acreage atop the cliffs—and in 1909 Palisades Interstate Park was dedicated.

From its southern extreme at Fort Lee, New Jersey to the New York State border, the park is more than 10 miles long, mostly under a mile wide—and almost entirely vertical. Beginning at the Englewood Boat Basin, just north of the graceful George Washington Bridge, the Shore Path winds among the fallen boulders at the foot of the cliffs. In places, steep, sharply elbowed trails lead to the Long Path, also paralleling the river, along the crest of the Palisades. It all depends on how you take your scenery: the broad sweep of the river and the New York skyline dominate the view from the overlooks on the Long Path, while the Shore Path walker is right at the water's edge, eyes usually cast up at the dark basalt brow. The Shore Path, which I have always preferred, is also more generous with half-forgotten sites accessible only to the foot traveler: the forlorn little graveyard that recalls the days of a colonial settlement called "Under the Mountain," or the melancholy stone ruins of the formal garden structures that marked the river entrance to a bygone estate. Also along the Shore Path is the sturdy white farm house in which Gen. Cornwallis set up headquarters during his pursuit of the Continental Army, recently routed from New York. The

Above: The Palisades and George Washington Bridge.
Right: Bear Mountain Bridge viewed from the top of Bear Mountain.

rebels were just out of reach, having evacuated Fort Lee with their campfires still burning. If there had been one wrong move or a moment's hesitation as the retreat across New Jersey began, the Union Jack might well be flying today over the entrances to the George III Bridge.

Major Andre's doom

Another crucial "might have been" episode of the American Revolution was played out to its sad conclusion just a few miles inland from the Palisades, in the Dutch village of Tappan that sits astride the state line. It was in Tappan, during Washington's bivouac at the DeWitt Mansion there in 1780, that the commander in chief entrusted Benedict Arnold with the defense of West Point. No sooner had Arnold received his command than he contacted the British commander in New York, Sir Henry Clinton, with an offer to betray the stronghold. Clinton sent his adjutant-general, Maj. John

Andre, to meet Arnold at Stony Point and work out the details. Andre kept his rendezvous with Arnold but he never returned to New York. On his way back down the valley, Andre was captured at Tarrytown, and the plans of West Point along with documents incriminating Arnold were found tucked into one of his boots., Arnold, when he heard of the apprehension, made good his escape beyond British lines in Manhattan. He was never captured and eventually even fought as a British officer. But the 29-year-old Andre was imprisoned, tried and convicted as a spy. He spent his last hours under guard in a Tappan tavern that still stands and was hanged on the second of October, 1780. "Bear witness to the world," he said after placing the noose around his neck, "that I die like a brave man." The place where the gallows stood is still called Andre Hill. The young officer was buried there, too, but in 1821 his remains were sent to Westminster Abbey.

Along the Tappan Zee

Just above Sneden's landing, where Cornwallis disembarked with his pursuit forces in 1776, the Hudson widens to form the Tappan Zee. "Cold spring sea" is the translation of the Indian and Dutch words that make up the name, and while it is hard to tell which cold springs the early inhabitants may have had in mind, there can be little doubt why the term "sea" seemed appropriate: at the point where a span of the New York Thruway crosses the Hudson on the Tappan Zee Bridge, the distance between Tarrytown and South Nyack is nearly three miles. Driving across the bridge is like traversing a huge, elongated lake that tapers southward toward the distant Manhattan skyline. On fine breezy days, the rippled surface of the "sea" is dotted with dozens of sailboats, dallying where once the serious business of commercial sloop traffic was carried out under snapping canvas.

Just north of Nyack, a town noted as the birthplace of the painter Edward Hopper as well as for rhyming with "kayak" in the song "Let's Get Away From It All," the Tappan Zee constricts between Croton Point, on the east, and the gently rounded promontory of Verdrietege Hook, on the west. Verdrietege Hook was named because of the nemesis headwinds faced by those early sailors, for whom negotiating this part of the river between the Tappan Zee and Haverstraw Bay was anything but a Saturday's lark. "Vertrietege" translates from the Dutch as "tedious," and we can imagine that stronger words were used on the umpteenth tack around the hook.

It isn't all that bad a trip to make on foot now that most of the hook between Nyack and Haverstraw is part of Palisades Interstate Park. This area, too, came under state protection because of the depredations of the quarrying industry, which was responsible for radically alternating the sharp, vertical lines of the diabase cliffs before dynamiting ended at the turn of the century.

But the slopes of Hook Mountain still rise steeply above the Hudson, and the 729-foot summit offers splendid views of the Tappan Zee, Croton Point and Haverstraw Bay, as well as

of the succession of ridges and lakes that lie to the west. Heading north, the footpath that parallels the river ascends the succession of smaller hills known as the Seven Sisters, and a less strenuous trail follows the Tappan Zee at water level. Along with the portion of the Palisades that extends south of the border into New Jersey and the Tallman Mountain Park on the river above Sneden's Landing, the heights along Verdrietege Hook comprise one of the earliest, most

A photographer's tribute to a painter of windows and light: at Edward Hopper's boyhood home in Nyack.

71

important and most successful attempts at preservation of the natural landscape near any large American urban area.

Another small section of Palisades Interstate Park, beginning at 832-foot High Tor just south of Haverstraw, illustrates the curvature of the sill-and-dike diabase formation of the Palisade cliffs westward away from the river toward what geologists call the "Ramapo Front." Beyond Verdrietege Hook, the 190-million-year-old "*sill*" (the hardened remnant of a horizontal irruption of magma into older sediment) changes into a "*dike*," which represents a similar intrusion of molten rock in a vertical direction.

At the northern extreme of Haverstraw Bay is a tiny link in the Palisades Interstate Park chain that was set aside for historic reasons, rather than because of the scenery created by the geological violence of 200 million years past. Stony Point is a lovely spot thrusting out sharply below the lazy S-curve that brings the Hudson south out of its dramatic gorge, but the 1,200 American troops that struck out from the promontory on July 6, 1779 were not here to enjoy the view. Their commander, Gen. "Mad" Anthony Wayne, had been charged by Washington with the capture of the British position on the heights of Stony Point. According to legend, when the commander in chief asked Wayne if he thought the operation feasible, Mad Anthony answered that he would "storm hell, sir, if you make the plans." Washington, the story goes, suggested that Wayne try Stony Point first. The impetuous officer was wounded during his successful assault on the British fort, but his men carried him over the ramparts to victory and eventual recovery; for the time being, he was spared an attempt at the more ambitious campaign he had rashly posed to his commander.

Harriman's legacy, Bear Mountain and the Hudson Highlands

While a series of baronial mansions dominate the river shore along the east bank of the Hudson, the west bank is characterized by its magnificent string of state parks. Curiously enough, an immense portion of the Palisades Interstate Park system is itself the legacy of a railroad titan who was no amateur when it came to mansion building—except in his case, his family kept the house and gave away the bulk of the land. His name was Edward Henry Harriman—as in Harriman the town on Route 17, Harriman State Park and W. Averill Harriman, his son the diplomat and governor of New York—and no man ever controlled more miles of American railroads.

E.H. Harriman was a minister's son who began his career as a clerk in a Wall Street brokerage. He could have done very well for himself moving paper rather than trains, but a taste of railroad management gained during the successful reorganization of an upstate New York operation set him about his life's work. His first major acquisition was the Illinois Central, but the real keystone of his success was his takeover of the badly ailing Union Pacific (UP)—a road disdained by no less an authority than J.P. Morgan as a "streak of rust" barely 20 years after its triumphal transcontinental link with the Central Pacific at Promontory, Utah. Harriman revitalized the UP, and then went on to acquire the vast Southern Pacific system and a slew of lesser roads. Perhaps the only man he could not outspend and outmaneuver was the fearsome James J. Hill of the Great Northern, and it was not for lack of trying. At the peak of his career, Harriman nonchalantly told a congressional committee that were he allowed to do so, he would go on buying up roads until the nation's entire rail network was in his hands. The man was a trustbuster's nightmare, but at least he believed in sound organization and the long-term health of his companies. Unlike Jay Gould, who ruled his pirate's empire from his Tarrytown mansion "Lyndhurst," E.H. Harriman did not buy railroads and gut them merely to line his own pockets.

Of course Harriman's pockets would end up very nicely lined anyway, and although he was not by nature a flamboyant man he set about building one of the most extravagant private residences in New York State. Having pieced together a 20,000-acre estate, "Arden," near the town of that name in Orange County, he crowned the Ramapo Range with a 150-room French Renaissance chateau surrounded by formal gardens. The house was finished in 1906, at a cost of $2 million—but Harriman did not have long to enjoy it. He died in 1909, aged 61, leaving his wife the house, the land and $100 million. In accordance with his wishes, she donated the eastern portion of the estate, some 11,000 acres, to the state of New York. (The house is still private.) The bequest became Harriman State Park, which combines with the adjacent Bear Mountain State Park to form the largest component of Palisades Interstate Park.

The Harriman-Bear Mountain unit of the park is a forest preserve and public recreation facility worthy of an

Empire State. Its southern boundary is at Suffern, near the New Jersey border, and it extends northeastward along either side of the beautiful Seven Lakes Drive toward the Hudson at Dunderberg and Bear Mountain. Dunderberg, which looms 920 feet above the river, was the "Thunder Mountain" of New Netherland: superstitious Dutch sailors believed that its fastnesses were the abode of the Heer, the capricious storm goblin that set off harrowing summer downpours and rent the sky with thunder and lightning. (This was an alternative to the story of Henry Hudson and his men playing ninepins; the men of Peter Stuyvesant's day could never get their

Above: Resting at the top of Bear Mountain.
Facing page, top: *Fishing the Hudson at Englewood Cliffs, New Jersey.*
Bottom: *Bear Mountain Lodge.*

Of the U.S. Military Academy's 43,000 graduates, more than 90 percent graduated since 1900.

Right: *At the Goshen trotting track.*
Far right: *Goshen town hall, where lexicographer Noah Webster once taught.*

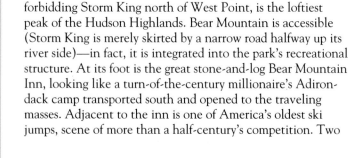

miles to the west, off Seven Lakes Drive, an auto road winds toward the 1,305-foot summit of Bear Mountain. But depending on what time of day or year you ascend Bear Mountain, the paved road and the observation tower and drop-in-a-dime swivel-mounted binoculars need not detract from the otherwise wild character of the surroundings. I drove to the top at about 6 p.m. one late spring day; it was the end of a gray, drizzly afternoon. The rain had finally stopped, and the newly budded May woods glistened. A deer stood alongside the road near the summit; later, two others crossed in front of the car. I got out at the top and walked across the rocks, able to make out only the misty outlines of the east and west shores of the Hudson below. As I stood there, though, the veil of mist began to dissipate in the deep clove beneath the mountain. As it rose, I could begin to discern the river's contours and to look deeper and deeper into the clove. There at the foot of Bear Mountain was a Hudson River School painting, a lesson in the power of this scenery to move the artists who took its name and made it famous in the world beyond the valley. The secret is not the sheer loftiness of the mountains—it is their precipitousness, and the variety of distances the eye encompasses within so short a range.

"The Gibraltar of America"

The phrase was George Washington's, and he used it to describe the stark shoulder of rock that forces the Hudson to bend abruptly to the east before flowing south through the Highlands. To Washington, however, the similarity of this

meteorological facts straight.) But no Heer was necessary to endanger the ships and crews that sailed the Hudson between Dunderberg and Bear Mountain—the Race, as it was called, is the narrowest part of the navigable river and the trickiest to navigate under sail.

Bear Mountain itself is the park's pinnacle, and, save for forbidding Storm King north of West Point, is the loftiest peak of the Hudson Highlands. Bear Mountain is accessible (Storm King is merely skirted by a narrow road halfway up its river side)—in fact, it is integrated into the park's recreational structure. At its foot is the great stone-and-log Bear Mountain Inn, looking like a turn-of-the-century millionaire's Adirondack camp transported south and opened to the traveling masses. Adjacent to the inn is one of America's oldest ski jumps, scene of more than a half-century's competition. Two promontory with Gibraltar was more than merely geological. Like the British fortress at Spain's southern tip, the rocky heights of West Point commanded a vital waterway, one that Washington had to control if the British were to be prevented from isolating New England from the Middle Atlantic colonies. Thus the Herculean chain stretched between the Point and the American defenses at Constitution Island, on the east bank of the river; thus the fortification of West Point itself, after the British withdrew from the area in the wake of their defeat at Saratoga. This was the installation entrusted to Benedict Arnold in 1780, which Arnold sought to hand over to the enemy when his loyalties shifted or his sense of loyalty evaporated. West Point remained in American hands throughout the remainder of the Revolution, but was destined for a continuing fame that far outstripped its wartime importance.

Public and congressional sympathy for a standing army was at a low ebb in the early years of the republic, and support for the training of professional military officers was similarly disregarded. These were European notions, part and parcel of the imperial order against which the colonies had rebelled. But pacific inclinations notwithstanding, the United States had no shortage of potential enemies as the 19th century began. In 1802, three years after his death, George Washington's hoped-for national service academy was finally voted into existence by Congress. It was to be located at West Point, one of only two army installations left active at the close of the Revolution.

The earliest years of the United States Military Academy were uncertain ones, plagued by chronic underfunding and a continuing absence of popular support for professional military training. An "officer caste" was suspect—but was of such undisputed usefulness in the Mexican and Civil wars (in the latter conflict, the top ranks of both sides were filled by West Pointers) that the Academy was never again threatened with outright abolition or slow financial strangulation. Still, West Point at the beginning of this century was still a far smaller institution than the one that straddles the heights overlooking the Hudson today: of its more than 43,000 graduates, more than 90 percent have graduated since 1900. It was, of course, the two world wars and their impact on the United States' role in the world that created the climate for the Academy's exponential growth.

Graduation ceremonies at West Point.

Top: *Washington's headquarters at Newburgh, the northern limit of the Hudson Highlands.*
Right: *Cannons seized by the U.S. in the Mexican War, at Trophy Point.*

The nation and the world have come a long way from the time when even the existence of a standing army might be questioned.

And yet for all the physical and educational changes at the Academy, all the buildings that have been built and curricular additions that have been made over the past two centuries in the place that graduated Grant and Lee, Eisenhower and MacArthur, the riverfront prospects that explain its being there in the first place have altered little. Stand at Trophy Point with your back to the Parade Ground, looking north to Newburgh Bay, and the sheer imperative of defending this spot in the reference frame of classical tactics strikes home in a way that transcends practical awareness that such things do not matter anymore. Canada and New England lie in one direction, the port of New York in the other, and the heights above this wasp-waist in the river command all.

With all its cadenced busy-ness, and all the martial clamor of its past, West Point is oddly one of the most tranquilly beautiful places from which to enjoy the presence of the river: the view of the opposite shore, after all, is of a sylvan stretch interrupted only by quaint Garrison's Landing. One evening I sat at a window table in the bar of the Thayer Hotel, a fortresslike Gothic lodgement on Academy property, and watched darkness fall on the reluctant Hudson. Because of its great breadth—even along this "narrow" stretch it is easily half a mile across—the river holds and reflects light long after the surrounding hills are lost in shadows; a milky twilight sheen remains on the surface of the water. Boats stand out in this prolonged half-light, as do pinpricks of illumination on shore. It is always special, in this dim but pervasive river light, to see the white shine of a sail in the distance.

Storm King to Woodstock

State Route 218 is the scenic pathway north from West Point. Unlike 9W, it holds closely to the river, ascending the east face of Storm King along a rocky shelf so narrow that one wonders how the builders managed to provide any turnoffs for viewing. This is, arguably, the most dramatic stretch of two-lane blacktop in the valley. Having rounded the mountain above a sheer drop to the shore, the road turns with the Hudson as it snakes west and widens into Newburgh Bay. For seven miles below and beyond, the river reaches for more than a mile between the steep Hudson Highlands.

Storm King was not always accorded such a portentous title. Henry Hudson named it "Klinkersberg" because of the way its broken rock face glistened in the sun, and throughout the 18th and much of the 19th centuries it was known even more prosaically by the name "Butter Hill," presumably because of its resemblance to a lump of butter. "Storm King" was the deliberate invention of a local poet named Nathaniel Willis, just over a hundred years ago. Perhaps he wished that a mountain with a good, fierce Anglo-Saxon name might steal some of Dunderberg's thunder.

Newburgh, along with the city of Beacon opposite, marks the northern limit of the Highlands proper. Once a lively port and actually an inland outpost of the whaling industry, Newburgh is a place bearing an almost melancholy sense of its past being greater than its present. The downtown streets are a trove of splendid 19th-century architecture—from Federal and Greek Revival to Italianate, Carpenter Gothic and the last of the century's fervent attempts at

At Newburgh.

Downtown Newburgh is a trove of 19th-century architectural treasures.

historicity—but the restorers' bills will be enormous. My own great-grandmother was born in Newburgh in 1850, and I suspect that as a girl she saw a town closer to its apogee than the one we see today.

A vigorous industry is centered on the west side of the river north of Newburgh that was hardly heard of in these parts when great-grandmother was young, although it surely must have had an amateur following. Now no fewer than 11 wineries are strung along the west shore between Newburgh and Kingston, including a couple just to the west in New Paltz; this makes the region second only to the Finger Lakes area in concentration of working vineyards. (Scatterings of wineries also are found on the east shore and in the southern Catskills). Virtually all of them run a brisk sideline in touring

Benmarl Vineyards at Marlboro.

rootstocks as a grafting medium. Along with French hybrids (to which, ironically, Dr. Frank himself was energetically opposed), the cultivation of *vinifera* strains has put the New York wine industry on the map. The Hudson Valley wines are not yet in the front rank of American or even New York labels, although several operations show considerable promise. In general, the whites are better than the reds.

The village of West Park, across the Hudson roughly from where Frederick Vanderbilt built his mansion, was for many years the home of one of America's most famous naturalists and apostles of conservation. John Burroughs was born in the Catskills town of Roxbury in 1837 (the railroad tycoon Jay Gould, born there a year earlier, was a classmate of Burroughs at Roxbury's one-room schoolhouse), and settled in his new stone house "Riverby" above the Hudson at West Park in 1873. Here, in a detached study overlooking the river, he wrote many of the 25 books and numerous essays that placed him in the ranks of his contemporary John Muir as an interpreter of man's relationship with the natural world. The civilized world, however, was hot on Burroughs' trail; his success as an author brought a steady flow of visitors to Riverby. The "lion hunters," he called them, and in an attempt to elude them Burroughs in 1895 built a two-story log cabin called "Slabsides" in the woods a mile and a half from his house. Here the lion might think, and write, and even tend to more prosaic interests: Burroughs made all of the cabin's rustic furniture himself.

Burroughs could never make good his escape, but at least the character of the lion hunters who sought him out at Slabsides must have made for stimulating conversation. The naturalist's friend Theodore Roosevelt came to visit in a government launch; other guests included Thomas Edison and Henry Ford—the latter a camping buddy of Burroughs' who gave him a Model T, which he learned to drive when he was 75 years old. What did those two talk about—the one a voice for the wild American landscape, and the other the inventor of the means by which nearly all of it would eventually be penetrated and subdued?

The town of New Paltz, west of the Hudson at the gateway to the Shawangunk Mountains, first strikes a visitor as a vestige of an era, a couple of decades back, that embraced the likes of John Burroughs, rejected the likes of Henry Ford and produced a culture that neither of them would have recognized. It looks, in short, as if it were freeze-dried in 1969, tie-dye shop and all. A

and sampling, which makes for an interesting approach to an exploration of the valley.

Although New York has grown to become the second largest wine producing state in the Union (California, of course, is first), connoisseurs for years disdained the local production as exhibiting the "foxiness" associated with native Concord grapes, or wrote off New York wines as cloyingly sweet, like certain Kosher wines in which the addition of sugar has nothing to do with religious observation. But today's consumers can enjoy a far more sophisticated product, thanks in large part to the efforts of the late Dr. Konstantin Frank, a Russian vintner of German parentage who settled in the Finger Lakes region. Dr. Frank was the first winemaker to demonstrate the feasibility of raising the European wine grape *vitis vinifera* in New York State, using cold-hardy local

Is it old Dutch magic that has freeze-dried New Paltz in its 1960s counterculture look?

possible explanation is the state college at New Paltz, but other college towns have long since started to look as if the 1970s and 1980s had passed. Who knows? Perhaps some old Dutch magic is at work here, some fey reversal of the Rip Van Winkle story that put the whole town, and not just one citizen, to sleep.

Even more remarkable proof that some preservative sorcery is at work in New Paltz is evident at a place called Huguenot Street, celebrated as "the oldest street in America." To be specific, it is the oldest street in the country that is still graced by its original houses. They are solid yet graceful gray stone houses, built in the last decade of the 17th century and the first decade of the 18th by French Huguenot refugees who came to this area by way of the Rhineland Palatinate—specifically, the area called *die Pfalz*, hence New Paltz. Stone houses do not age at all; to walk down Huguenot Street, eyes

A Huguenot stone house at New Paltz, and a relaxed denizen of the town.

Right and far right: *Woodstock present and past.*

craftspeople and musicians (the pink house referred to in the Band's album title "Music from Big Pink" is located near Woodstock) had been gravitating to the town for years and they still do. But Woodstock, which is situated just northwest of Kingston about nine miles west of the Hudson, is so close to the main ski-and-summer-tourist routes that it has inevitably commercialized and atrophied into something resembling a hip strip mall. On a drive along its long, curving main street—the only street in town of any substance—I counted more than 30 small establishments dealing in such things as stained glass, kitchen supplies, pottery, magic paraphernalia, bagels, health foods, ceramic tiles and the rest of the normal run of small-town necessities. (I did not, however, see anyplace where one might buy a screwdriver or a mop.) Even on a day in March, when the last of the year's skiing had retreated to the far Adirondacks and the green scent of spring was no closer than south Jersey, kids who were barely ambulatory at the time of the Bethel Festival were slouching along the strip and working hard at looking cool—not in the hard-edged, hot-pastel style of the late 1980s, but earthtoned and slack-maned, like the Rip Van Winkles of New Paltz. Going to Woodstock is like going to Williamsburg and knowing you are going to see three-cornered hats and knee breeches to complement the Georgian architecture.

The "real" Catskills

Woodstock might well be taken as the gateway to the Catskills. To the modern understanding, of course, the town is

diverted from automobiles, is to walk in the Hudson Valley in the year 1710. And as a fillip to this time warp, you can hike a few blocks to buy incense and a frozen yogurt.

When it comes to conjuring memories of the counterculture, though, the real magic word is not New Paltz but Woodstock. This is the result of one of recent history's most blatant misnomers: the great music festival of August 1969 was to have been held in Woodstock, but the venue was changed almost at the last minute to Bethel, a tiny farm town 50 miles away in the southwestern Catskills. The fact that Joni Mitchell did not name her song "Bethel" (same syllabication, though) just helped to make the error permanent. But—Woodstock wasn't really a place, was it?

Well, Woodstock was and is a place, a place with a certain arty cachet even before the festival. Artists, way up *in* the Catskills: nowadays, people use the term loosely to cover virtually all the territory between the Delaware and the Hudson rivers, from the Jersey line north nearly to Albany. The sprawling hotels of the "Borscht Belt"—places such as Grossinger's, the Concord and the Nevele, which grew from farmhouse accommodations popular with Jewish New Yorkers into the lavish resorts that incubated modern American comedy—are mostly clustered off Route 17, closer to Pennsylvania than to the mountains that rise north of Woodstock, yet they are always referred to as being in the "Catskills." (The etymology has never been established for sure, at least beyond "kill" for stream.) The region is also commonly understood to include the northeast-southwest ridge of the Shawangunks (pronounced "Shon-gums" but usually abbreviated to "Gunks,") on which generations of rock climbers have honed their skills. Actually, the eastern portion of Catskill State Park, with Woodstock on its southern border, more closely corresponds to the old Dutch understanding of what constituted the Catskills and to general American agreement as recently as the late 19th century. Here, and in the more westerly reaches of the park, are peaks that dwarf the Hudson Highlands: Slide Mountain, 4,204 feet; Hunter Mountain, 4,025 feet; Black Dome, 3,990 feet; West Kill Mountain, 3,925 feet; and Doubletop, 3,905 feet, are just a few. One part of these "classical" Catskills, roughly surrounding Tannersville, is indeed so rigorously mountainous that it was long dubbed simply the "Mountain Top." But the connotation of a single, mesa-like aerie that this term carries is misleading. The *haute* Catskills constitute a sharply riven landscape of great humped domes, steep-sided and separated by deep cloves. The visual drama of this terrain is contained not only in its tortuous verticality, but in the play of light and shadow it creates: a road might easily turn and dip into the bottom of a pass so shaded from the day that the effect is gloomy, almost melancholy; at dusk, it can be downright spooky. The folk imagination that had such a field day with storm-producing goblins in the Hudson Highlands must really have been put in awe of the Catskills. Not surprisingly, Palenville, on the eastern edge of the Mountain Top, was Washington Irving's model for the hometown of Rip Van Winkle.

One odd aspect of the Catskills is that even though much, if not all, of this mystery should have been surrendered

Mohonk Mountain House at Lake Mohonk is the last of the luxurious Catskills behemoths.

long ago, given the popularity of the region with tourists, it has not. The most visible aspect of the Catskills' draw to outsiders today is the ski industry. But as land-intensive, and socially and environmentally disruptive, as big-time downhill skiing can be, it somehow seems to sit lightly on these hills. While enormous facilities such as Hunter (private) and Bellayre (one of the few state-run ski areas in the nation, and arguably the finest) do take up their share of mountain acreage and have spawned the usual secondary enterprises— motels, restaurants, jerrybuilt nightclubs—it is nevertheless still possible to drive the back roads of the Mountain Top in the off-season and feel as if you are in the middle of nowhere.

Summer tourism is far older than skiing in the Catskills. In fact, the Mountain Top district was perhaps the first real "resort" area in the United States, attracting visitors who would travel upriver from New York to enjoy the scenery that

likewise inspired our first important native school of painters. Artists and tourists arrived more or less at the same time. Thomas Cole, founder of the Hudson River School, first came to the Catskills in 1825, while the preceding year had seen the building of the Catskill Mountain House, soon to become one of the nation's most prestigious summer resorts. The three-story wooden hotel, with its colonnaded portico and veranda commanding a majestic sweep of mountain and Hudson River scenery, remained open for nearly 120 years, and stood until, finally derelict, it was acquired and deliberately burned by the New York State Department of Conservation in 1967. The day of the luxurious arks that catered to clients staying weeks or even months at a time is as gone in the Catskills as it is virtually everywhere else. The only survivor of the breed in these parts is the palatial Mohonk Mountain House, a national historic landmark that has stood for more than a century atop a rocky outpost of the Shawangunks above New Paltz.

As beautifully appointed and gloriously situated as the Catskill Mountain House was, a smaller local establishment, the Laurel House, was able to boast that it was built almost directly above the Mountain Top's single most spectacular natural feature: Kaaterskill Falls, New York State's highest waterfall.

No broad Niagara, but more a miniature version of Angel Falls in Venezuela, Kaaterskill leaps from a rock ledge as a narrow curtain of white water, plunging past a natural grotto to a second scooped-out shelf at which it gathers force to finish its plunge toward the floor of Kaaterskill Clove. Now little celebrated outside of hikers' guidebooks (a *New Yorker* writer once claimed to have spent the better part of two summers trying to locate the falls, although at least one readily available guide could have put her at the top or bottom within minutes of leaving Tannersville), Kaaterskill Falls was once the Catskills' most celebrated natural wonder. It not only lured sightseers to the now-vanished Laurel House, which maintained a walkway with protective railings right to the edge of the precipice; it was a special attraction for the painters who frequented the region. Thomas Cole was the first, with his *View of Kaaterskill Falls*, and so many others followed that the scene eventually became familiar enough to serve as a subject for Currier and Ives.

I set out to reach the falls on a bright day in late March, when old snow still lay deep in the shadowy recesses of Kaaterskill Clove. Route 23A follows the clove west out of Palenville; rising sharply, the road bends to form a fiddler's elbow roughly five miles east of Tannersville. Here is the beginning of the trail to Kaaterskill Falls. It is not a particularly difficult path, although in the spring of the year when its snow cover has melted and refrozen into glare ice it requires a gingerly step, but it is a short trail. It follows the ravine gouged by Kaaterskill Creek for less than a mile before reaching the base of the falls.

The snow deepened, and bridges of ice covered more and more of the creek as I trudged closer to the spot where the falls comes into view. What I saw when I got there was not Cole's ideal verdant wilderness rent by the cataract, but more a vision out of some Nordic tale of ice fairies. At my feet was a stream rushing noisily beneath a solid bridge of ice and snow, while above—beyond the falls' half-way shelf—a cone of ice ascended to receive the meltwater-swollen creek as it rushed over the topmost rim. It was a waterfall truncated and tunnelized, its sheerest and most magnificent drop temporarily concealed by the freezing of its own wall of mist. I decided to try the view from the top, which entailed a half-hour scramble up a steep slope of loose, wet scree beneath a fast-disintegrating palisade of enormous icicles. I reached level ground and walked to the cluster of boulders that form the lip of Kaaterskill Falls, only to find a loud gaggle of 17-year-olds who had walked there on level ground from a state park parking lot a few hundred yards away. Places like this should not be accessible from the top, I decided. I crept to the

edge of the rocks and looked into the blue maw of ice that swallowed the cataract, and then backed off a few yards to read the ancient graffiti chipped into the biggest boulder at the head of the falls. The oldest carving I saw was "E.H.-1825." That was the year Thomas Cole first came to the Mountain Top, but I could not find any "T.C."

The last miles to Albany

Thomas Cole did eventually settle in these parts, not on the Mountain Top itself, but in the old town of Catskill that the Dutch had established where Kaaterskill Creek meets the Hudson. The English-born painter's house on Spring Street still stands, and has become something of an attraction in its own right. It is no Olana, but then again Cole did not live as long, nor did he enjoy the same commercial success, as did his protégé Church. (Cole died at age 47 in 1848, before the heated midcentury economy made possible the kind of prices Church's work would command.) The Catskill that Cole knew, like Saugerties and Kingston on the Hudson to the south, was a lively shipbuilding town, perfectly situated to take advantage of river traffic as well as overland shipping from the farms and villages to the west. The Susquehanna Turnpike, roughly paralleling the course of modern Route 23, skirted the northern Catskills and brought settlements as far west as the Pennsylvania border in contact with the river at Catskill. Catskill milled upstate wheat and sent it downstream to New York City; Saugerties tanned leather with bark

Above: Refreshing Schoharie Creek in Catskill Park.
Left: A Flag Day ceremony at Kingston.
Facing page, left: Kaaterskill Falls—the reward at the end of a difficult trail.
Right: The Old Senate House at Kingston, where New York state government began in 1777.

83

Above: The new and the old side by side at Lexington.
Right: New England–style charm at Jewett.

stripped from Catskills trees and built fast steamboats; Kingston, after 1828, was the eastern terminus of the Delaware and Hudson Canal and an important transshipment point for Pennsylvania anthracite.

Kingston's political day in the sun passed a half century before the canal was dug. From February to October of 1777, the town was effectively the capital of New York. Here, in the building now known as the Senate House, the state's constitution was approved and the first governor inaugurated under the new document's provisions. The legislature held session at Kingston until just nine days before the northward-advancing British arrived and burnt the village.

The decline of the small river cities after the advent of the railroad is an old and oft-repeated story, a story that well describes the situation of Kingston, Saugerties, and Catskill. Catskill's troubles actually began even before the tracks came up the valley—when the Erie Canal was finished, the commercial traffic that supported the Susquehanna Turnpike gravitated north toward the new, cheaper water route. Eventually, though, the railroads did have their say, extinguishing the viability of canals and canal towns as surely as canals had made the old turnpikes obsolete. The Delaware and Hudson Canal may have been a good way to move coal from Pennsylvania to Kingston, but once that coal started burning in the fireboxes of locomotives on the West Shore Railroad, the Erie, and the Delaware, Lackawanna & Western, the days of mules pulling barges from lock to lock at a snail's pace were over.

And so the appearance of the old river settlements: faded advertisements painted on the side walls of Italianate brick buildings, touting businesses remembered by no one now alive; here or there a derelict brickyard, or icehouse, or wooden pier; an 1874 lighthouse on a little island between Hudson and Athens, built to serve a river thick with fast steamers even as their era came to a close, and today winking caution at immense barges stopping nowhere between the great cities at either end of the valley. In Coxsackie stand stone houses and even a tavern built in the old step-gabled Dutch fashion; and the brick downtown streets of Saugerties looks as if they just sent their sons off to the Civil War. Athens, another place where the sloops and steamers call no more, has painted and repointed its way beyond dilapidation. Athens is a tiny town in which the Hudson laps at the backyards, and on which time sits not as it does on an abandoned house but upon a period parlor preserved in a

Rustic scenes of the Catskills.

museum. Down by the waterfront I saw workmen restoring an old hotel—they had the first floor finished, and it was done up smartly as a 19th-century tavern.

Taverns—taverns and roadhouses and small-town saloons—these are among the salient memories of the byways and settlements of the Hudson Valley, especially along the west shore. The sheer numbers of these places and the shortness of the distance between them is no reflection on the drinking habits of New Yorkers, who probably imbibe no more than any other geographical grouping of Americans, but their survival says something about how the valley developed and how it sometimes clings oddly to its past. I have my own theories as to why this part of the country is a last holdout of the roadhouse—a term I use not in its honky-tonk but its quiet tavern sense. The Hudson Valley has long been a place

not only of deep-rooted settlements but of movement, of passage by road and water between small towns and great cities. The drivers and passengers of stagecoaches, and the bargemen, canalboatmen and river sailors who moved the young republic's goods along, depended on a tradition of innkeeping as old as mercantile civilization. The old thirsty legacy of hardworking Yankees and Dutchmen was never erased hereabouts, not by Prohibition nor by the postwar sanitization of our national habits. (In New England, a traveler nowadays will more likely take refreshment in the tap room of an apotheosized country inn, complete with $7 hamburgers.) And so the Hudson Valley taverns survive, not so much as places to tank up for disaster but merely as shady spots to have a glass of ale and maybe, if it is in view, to watch the river slowly drift from Albany down through time.

The sloop Clearwater.

CHRIS MAYNARD

Learn what we may about the land that lies along either side of the Hudson, about its history and its people and its lore, the fact remains that the central presence of the valley is the river itself. Not as a pathway to settlement, nor as an artery of commerce, nor as a shimmering foil to the beauties of the Highlands does the Hudson ultimately figure most importantly, but as a living body of water that draws sustenance from the land around it and gives back life in return. Any limited compartmentalization of our understanding of the river—whether as a subject in art history or as a factor in industrial waste management—will ultimately diminish that life. For generations the people of the valley have needed the Hudson, and they still do; today, the Hudson needs their attention as well.

How healthy is the Hudson River? We know that for upwards of three and a half centuries, its banks have supported an ever-growing human population, and that for nearly half that time the towns and cities along the valley have been industrialized. Neither of these factors amounts to a recipe for clean water, and the depredations they have led to have been well chronicled in books such as Robert H. Boyle's *The Hudson River,* in countless magazine stories and in the reports of public and private environmental organizations. The portrayal has often been bleak: as Boyle points out, no river in the world has been more polluted with carcinogenic polychlorinated biphenyls (PCBs). We are also aware of the decades-long discharge of a deadly soup of other industrial contaminants, of the fish kills caused by the intake screens and thermal pollution associated with the cooling system of the nuclear power plant at Indian Point, and of the relentless discharge of untreated and partially treated sewage from cities and towns along the valley. All of it adds up to a river I was loathe to fall into when I paddled the canoe around Manhattan and, of course, to a thousand other less personally calamitous but far more insidious phenomena.

Fortunately the Hudson has its dedicated friends. One of the most tireless organizations devoted to the riverine environment is one that acts out of simple enlightened self-interest—the Hudson River Fishermen's Association (HRFA). People who have given up hope for the river, who still regard it as an environmental disaster that has already happened, forget that the Hudson is still healthy enough to support an estimated 150 species of fish, several of which remain important for commercial or sport purposes either in the river itself or in the ocean to which some species return after spawning in the river. The Hudson's commercial shad fishery survives, and sport fishing for this larger relative of the herring—famous for its delicate roe—is on the increase. Shad spawn in areas offshore from the towns of Kingston and Catskill. There is a small, but still marginally viable Atlantic sturgeon fishery in Haverstraw Bay; a century ago, these primitive giants were so heavily fished, and overfished, in the Hudson, that sturgeon was known as "Albany beef." (The shortnose sturgeon, which lives mostly in the estuarine portion of the river, is officially considered endangered and is no longer legally fished.) Black bass are still prolific in the Hudson, so much so that sport fishing for the species has even reached the point of annual tournaments in Columbia

A barge at the Newburgh Bridge.

County. While the remnants of the great oyster beds of the Tappan Zee can no longer be fished because of pollution, there is still some commercial taking of blue crabs near the mouth of the river, and as recently as the mid-1980s, there were 19 lobstermen licensed in New York City. The HRFA champions the interests of those who continue to make their livings on the river, and in the course of doing so has proved to be an effective investigator and sometime litigator of pollution-related issues. The organization, which even employs a "riverwatcher" assigned to patrol the Hudson by boat to keep an eye on things (John Cronin, who holds the position, was admirably profiled in a 1987 *New Yorker* article), has blown the whistle on illegal industrial discharges, oil company tankers that flush their tanks with river water, and even a ship that was siphoning the Hudson's water to transport to an arid resort island in the Bahamas.

The River's most famous sloop

By far the most publicly visible of all the organizations that study and safeguard the Hudson, though, is a group known simply as "Clearwater," after the beautiful sloop that is its most valuable educational tool and publicity vehicle.

The idea of the boat took shape before the idea of the organization. It started when Pete Seeger—folksinger, history buff, sailor and resident of Beacon, New York—read Collier and Verplanck's *Sloops of the Hudson* and began talking with friends about building a replica of one of the sleek sailing vessels that once worked the Hudson from one end to the

Above and right: *Aboard the* Clearwater.

Above: Enjoying the Kingston
waterfront.
Right: The Hudson and the
Palisades.
Facing page. Environmental
education for 20th-century people
aboard the 19th-century Clearwater.

other. As Seeger and his associates began raising money to build the sloop, the derisive remarks they heard about sailing on a river as dirty as the Hudson led them to the idea of using their boat as more than just a floating reminder of the past. It could, they decided, be put to work as the central focus of a river cleanup campaign. Thus began the Hudson River Sloop Clearwater, Inc., a non-profit organization dedicated to environmental research and education. *Clearwater's* keel was laid in Maine in 1968, and it made its maiden voyage up the Hudson in the summer of 1969. (An accurate replica of a classic 19th-century river sloop, it measures 106 feet in length with a mast height of 108 feet.) With that first sailing began the mission of reversing the decline of the Hudson River ecosystem, a mission that continues today.

The Clearwater organization's offices are in Poughkeepsie, and there I talked with Steve Stanne, a former volunteer crew-member who now organizes Clearwater's educational program.

"When *Clearwater* first sailed, she was seen primarily as a means of attracting attention back to the river," explained Stanne, a tall, athletic man in his 30s to whom an office seems a physical constraint and a computer a poor substitute for snapping canvas. "That was before the first Earth Day, before the Clean Water Act, when the public perception of the Hudson was of a sewer—and it wasn't far off. But by 1970 the boat had become a floating classroom, and in the following year our educational programs began full time."

Each year's sailing season finds *Clearwater* cruising the Hudson from New York harbor to Albany, hosting school field trips, scout and 4-H excursions, museum and library association outings, and visits by just about any group wishing to schedule a day sail. These trips upon the river are an adventure in environmental education, with volunteers assisting the professional crew in staffing a number of on-board learning stations.

"Typically, a class of schoolchildren on a half-day sail will break into smaller groups that rotate from station to station," said Steve Stanne. "We'll have a fish station, at which we haul up our trawl net and identify the species that live in the river; a station with microscopes for looking at plankton; a small lab setup for analyzing simple water chemistry; and a session on navigation in which kids learn the rudiments of chart reading and even get to handle the tiller. We take them below decks to see how the crew lives, and let them help raise our ton-and-a-half mainsail. And there are periods of silence, when these city children can just stand on deck listening to the sounds of an 19th-century boat on a 20th-century river."

During the two decades in which *Clearwater* the sloop and Clearwater the membership organization have evolved to fulfill the role envisioned by Pete Seeger and the other visionaries who launched them both, the singer-activist's own role has changed. "Pete Seeger doesn't like people thinking that it's his boat," Steve Stanne explained. "He emphasizes that it belongs to Clearwater's 10,000 members, and in fact he is seldom on board these days and no longer serves as a director. But he's as active as ever on the local level, which he feels is the most important." These days, Seeger uses his newer, smaller sloop, the *Woody Guthrie*, to inspire people to work on behalf of the river in the communities near his home.

As important as local organization is, however, numerous issues require a whole-river perspective, with constant monitoring and pressure at legislative, administrative and judicial levels if *Clearwater* is to be able to continue its educational mission upon a living waterway. I asked Steve Stanne about the major problems toward which Clearwater's researchers and lobbyists direct most of their attention, and gathered from his answers that activists along this river have more than enough to keep them busy to the end of the century and beyond.

Looming as large as any other single issue is the matter of pollutant discharges. The toxic chemicals that have received the most publicity and likely caused the most damage by lodging in living creatures throughout the food chain are PCBs and, although dumping has stopped, Stanne pointed out that "no one knows" how to get rid of the PCBs that were discharged into the river over the years. (The leading source was the General Electric complex at Hudson Falls and Fort Edward.) "The chemical is concentrated in several hotspots north of Troy," said Stanne. "In the 1970s, a state commission estimated that it would cost forty million dollars to dredge out these spots and put the contaminated sludge in a safe landfill. Twenty million has since been appropriated, but no town wants the landfill. Meanwhile, we still don't know how long PCBs take to break down, or whether they can slowly be degraded by bacteria in the river." What we do know is that fish such as striped bass have unacceptably high levels of PCBs—and the spawning grounds of the Hudson currently produce half of the stripers along the east coast. The commercial striped bass fishery on the river was closed in 1975 and commercial and recreational fisheries have since have been severely restricted as far out as eastern Long Island.

JIM CRONK

Water Act allows citizens to sue for proper enforcement of this legislation. Clearwater has been involved in several suits, both as a plaintiff and as *amicus curiae* in action initiated by the state against polluters."

Another problem area, in which there has been marked improvement, is that of sewage discharge. The Clean Water Act mandated sewage treatment and provided money for towns along the Hudson to build the necessary plants. The reduction in untreated sewage has not only helped the appearance of the river, but has allowed oxygen levels to increase to the benefit of fish populations. Still, progress has often been agonizingly slow. "As recently as 1986, New York City was still dumping 200 million gallons of raw sewage into the river and harbor each day," said Stanne. "Now there are two new primary plants to handle this flow, and it's hoped that by the early nineties all of the city's sewage output will be treated up to the secondary level."

Oil pollution has also been curtailed; stricter safeguards covering barge traffic and riverside tank farms have resulted in less spillage in oil cargo transfers.

Other issues affecting the river's ecology are as irrevocably linked to population pressures as the problem of sewage. One is the withdrawal of water from the river: Poughkeepsie and five smaller towns get their drinking water from the Hudson, and New York City wants to make permanent use of its emergency pumping station at Chelsea to draw up to 300 million gallons of river water per day to supplement its upstate reservoir supply. And development continues along the Hudson's shoreline. "As the river becomes cleaner, more people want houses, restaurants and marinas on its banks," Stanne explained. "As of early 1988, there are over 12,000 new units of housing proposed for land adjacent to the river between New York and Albany—and that's just in large developments. Open space and public access will be an increasingly crucial problem, as will increasing pollutant loads carried in stormwater runoff from urban streets."

The Hudson, then, is a river still caught between the dangers of neglect and the inevitable pressures that accompany rediscovery. In metaphor as well as in fact, it is still "the water that flows two ways" so aptly named by the Algonquins. Which way it flows into the 21st century will be a question largely answered through the work of activists such as those who make up the membership of Clearwater, and who sail its namesake sloop across the sullied yet resilient waters that pour from the Adirondacks into New York harbor.

As for ongoing discharges of other industrial pollutants, Stanne charged that "the system for controlling them should work, but the reality is different." He is referring to the State Pollution Discharge Elimination System (SPDES, pronounced "Speedies"), a scheme devised to limit ambient levels of various pollutants so that water quality may be improved and maintained. But enforcement is a continuing problem. A state SPDES permit, required for any industrial discharge, sets levels on the type and amount of any substance to be released into the river, and stipulates monitoring and reporting of these levels. However it is the companies to which the permits are issued that are responsible for holding to their terms; even though the state can make spot checks, the situation is essentially one of self-policing. With state budgeting and manpower perennially short, real enforcement of SPDES terms—and the levying and collecting of fines when those terms are not met—is frequently lacking. "There's a lack of political will," said Stanne. "But fortunately, the federal Clean

The Hudson River School

It fell upon one of the longest-settled parts of the New World to give its name to a school of painting that celebrated the rough glories of wilderness more reverently than any artists had before or have since. The Hudson River School, America's first coherent artistic movement, was born of the same reconsideration of the natural world as a fit subject for artistic expression that gave rise to romantic poetry. The school came along a little later—Thomas Cole's 1825 arrival in the Catskill Mountains postdated William Wordsworth's first wandering "lonely as a cloud" in the English Lake District by a good 30 years. But unlike poetry, which can admit to a good deal more imaginative elaboration than painting, the sheer naturalistic representation of wilderness on canvas had to await the discovery of scenes "commensurate with man's capacity for wonder," as F. Scott Fitzgerald eventually would describe Europeans' first perceptions of the New World in the closing lines of *The Great Gatsby*.

Of course, for two centuries before there was a Hudson River School, Europeans had been encountering a valley even wilder than the one eventually depicted by the mid-19th century painters. The Dutch sailors, as Fitzgerald reminded us, saw it first. But the builders of New Netherland and New York, and of the United States of America, were far too preoccupied with taming the wilderness to appreciate a place like the Hudson Valley in its natural incarnation. The built environment and the human condition concerned them more: had there been time and money for such things in the valley settlements of the 17th century, the Dutch burghers would likely have opted for paintings of themselves and their families in the wonderfully illuminated style bequeathed to civilization by their countrymen in Holland during the same period. Remember, "verdrietege" as in Verdrietege Hook does not mean breathtaking; it means tedious.

By the 1820s, aesthetics had taken a different turn. Painters could look upon the Hudson Highlands, or Newburgh Bay from West Point, or the Catskills from across the river at Hudson, and depict what they actually saw—not an idealized pastoral (although it is hard to imagine nettles or mosquitoes in a Hudson River School painting) but the sublimely beautiful wilderness that still existed up and down the valley. They saw a landscape that had survived the clearing and farming and town-building and steamboats to survive into an age that could afford the luxury, and appreciate the nostalgia, of seeing it for what it was.

Thomas Cole is generally recognized as the founder of the Hudson River School. Born in England in 1801, he emigrated to America with his family in 1818, worked at a variety of jobs including art teacher and portrait painter, and by the early 1820s had become enamored of the landscapes of the American artist Thomas Doughty. In 1825, Cole took that fateful first sketching trip upriver, past the Palisades and Highlands and into the Mountain Top region of the Catskills. Here, amidst the mountains he later described as heaving "from the valley of the Hudson like the subsiding billows of the ocean after a storm," Cole made pictures that were discovered, later that same year, by several of the leading artists and collectors of New York. Although he later painted European scenes, and eventually turned heavily toward allegorical and moralistic themes, the core of Cole's work as it has been appreciated by succeeding generations has always been his Hudson River canvases. These paintings did more than simply document the scenery of the valley; they helped bring into vogue a taste for a certain raw gorgeousness in the depiction of nature—a dizzying precipitousness, as in *Catskill Mountain House* or *View of Kaaterskill Falls*, or a reminder, as in *Catskill Creek*, that the apricot clouds and cerulean skies of an autumn sunset can seem

Facing page: "Border of the Brook" by John Frederick Kensett (1816-1872).

COURTESY OF THE VOSE GALLERIES OF BOSTON, INC.; PHOTOGRAPHED BY CLIVE RUSS

95

almost preternaturally beautiful in a picture until you remember that you have actually seen them that way, even if only once.

Thomas Cole's near-contemporary, Asher Brown Durand, was for years a portrait painter before turning to landscapes when he was nearly 40. Born in 1796, he outlived Cole by 38 years and died in 1886. A disciple of William Turner and a great believer in the supreme value of nature itself as a teacher, Durand once wrote that "true art teaches the use of the embellishments which nature itself furnishes, it never creates them." His Hudson River landscapes are rich in browns and deep greens tinged with the gold of diffused sunlight, and are unstinting in their provision of detail in the near and middle distance. One possible reason for such verisimilitude (and for the almost imperceptibly gradual hazing of elements far away) was Durand's habit of painting in oils on location, rather than making preliminary outdoor sketches from which to work in his studio. In a sense, Durand thus struck another blow for naturalism.

Two younger painters of the Hudson River School were responsible for helping to develop the style known as luminism, after its preoccupation with the effects of light conveyed through the atmosphere. John Frederick Kensett (1816-1872) and Jasper Cropsey (1823-1900) sought, in paintings such as Cropsey's *Upper Hudson* and Kensett's *Lakes and Mountains*, to establish a source of light that was at once nowhere and everywhere—that seemed to emanate from all points along a central horizontal swath of the canvas with the luminosity characteristic of days that are at once bright and hazy. Luminism eventually transcended the Hudson River School, accounting for the softly incandescent horizontal harbor and saltmarsh views of Martin Johnson Heade and Fitz Hugh Lane, but it may well be said to have begun in the valley.

The Hudson River School achieved the full voluptuousness that preceded its decline in the work of two of its most famous painters—Frederic Edwin Church, builder of Olana, and the German-born Albert Bierstadt. In a sense Church was in the direct artistic line of descent from the movement's founder, having been a student of Thomas Cole's for two years in the 1840s. But Church pressed beyond his mentor's approach to natural subjects in a way that made the older man's style seem almost chaste. The seasonal views of the Hudson, and the Catskills beyond, that Church painted as witnessed from the vantage of Olana are a testament not only to the region's scenery, but to feats of lighting so magnificent they could only

CHRIS MAYNARD PHOTOS BOTH PAGES

Hudson River School painters depicted the sublimely beautiful wilderness that still existed up and down the valley.

Left: *At the Benmarl Vineyards near Marlboro.*
Facing page: *A view along the path to Kaaterskill Falls is very much Hudson River School material.*

have been accomplished by Turner in a rare mood or Jehovah in a rarer. But interestingly enough, it was not his Hudson River work that set Church on the path to wealth and adulation, but the gigantic canvases *Heart of the Andes* and *Niagara*. Here, with the simultaneous eye for fine detail and appreciation of the dramatic sweep of a noble landscape that fired the movement he matured in, Church brought the old Hudson River values to the world beyond the valley.

Albert Bierstadt went several steps further, adopting the painterly techniques of the Hudson River School for the enormous task of chronicling the American West. Although he spent a good part of his life in Irvington-on-Hudson and painted local subjects, his reputation was made in the Sierra Nevada rather than on the Tappan Zee. In the mountains of the West, which he visited on several expeditions beginning in 1859, Bierstadt—and American art—finally met up with

the ultimate challenge to our capacity for wonder. A *Storm in the Rocky Mountains*, as Bierstadt saw it, was enough to make the rumblings around the Dunderberg pale by comparison. But after a scant two decades of success that paralleled Church's years of popularity, Bierstadt's enormous pictures and the whole preceding oeuvre of the Hudson River School fell into neglect if not outright disrepute. Americans had seen their wild landscapes and had enjoyed them most when they were fresh for the discovery. A new sophistication was in the air, and when the outdoors was invited in it was most welcome when depicted with the economy of a Winslow Homer. Before long anyone who wanted an exact picture of Yosemite's Half Dome or New York's Storm King could just go out and take one...but even George Eastman's best film wouldn't be up to delivering a Frederic Church sunset.

97

Right: *In the Little Westkill Valley, Greene County.*

Facing page: *"Lake George" by Asher B. Durand (1796-1886).*

JIM CRONK

Epilogue

Most American places do not feel
haunted…

CHRIS MAYNARD

It was a good two or three years after the time of Chris Maynard's and my canoe camp on the bridge over Spuyten Duyvil—some time, in fact, after I described that night and the sound of a crew singing in Dutch in the prologue to this book—that I turned up the story of the storm-ship in a hundred-year-old guidebook to the Hudson. It seems that in the days of Peter Stuyvesant, the villagers of New Amsterdam were surprised one evening to see a ship sail past the Battery and up the river against the wind; it disappeared beyond the Palisades and never was seen to return. But ever after, during stormy weather on Haverstraw Bay or the Tappan Zee, it was spotted out upon the waves, while during good weather it rode at anchor near the east bank above the Highlands. Especially around the time of the harvest moon, its sails stood out clearly against the night sky, and when the captain spoke orders to the crew the words that drifted across the water sounded to all like Low Dutch.

For Further Reading

Above: At Croton Reservoir.
Facing page: Early autumn in the Catskills. JIM CRONK

Biography of a River: The People and Legends of the Hudson Valley. By John Mylod. Ed. by Alec Thomas. New York: Hawthorn Books, 1969.

Chronicles of the Hudson: Three Centuries of Travelers' Accounts. Comp. by Roland Van Zandt. New Brunswick, N.J.: Rutgers University Press, 1971.

Country Walks Near New York. By William G. Scheller. Boston: Appalachian Mountain Club, 1986.

Fifty Hikes in the Hudson Valley. By Barbara McMartin and Peter Kick. Woodstock, VT: Backcountry Publications, 1985.

The Hudson. By Wallace Bruce. Centennial Edition. New York: Walking News, Inc., 1982. (Original edition published 1882, rev. 1907.)

The Hudson. By Carl Carmer. (Illustrated Rivers of America.) New York: Grosset & Dunlap, 1939, 1968.

The Hudson River: A Natural and Unnatural History. By Robert H. Boyle. New York: W.W. Norton & Co., 1979.

The Hudson River and Its Painters. By John K. Howat. New York: American Legacy Press, 1983.

Legends of the Shawangunk. By Philip H. Smith. Syracuse, NY: Syracuse University Press, 1965.

New York: A Guide to the Empire State. (American Guide Series.) Compiled by workers of the Writers' Program of the Work Projects Administration in the State of New York. New York: Oxford University Press, 1940.

New York: Off the Beaten Path. By William G. Scheller. Chester, CT: Globe Pequot Press, 1987.

O Albany! By William Kennedy. New York: Viking Penguin, 1983.

Rock Scenery of the Hudson Highlands and Palisades: A Geological Guide. By Jerome Wyckoff. Glens Falls, NY: Adirondack Mountain Club, 1971.

Westchester: Portrait of a County. By Alex Shoumatoff. New York: Coward, McCann & Geoghegan, 1979.

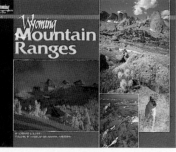

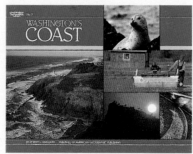